NEWCASTLE/BLOODAXE POETRY SERIES: 10

FIONA SAMPSON:
MUSIC LESSONS

NEWCASTLE/BLOODAXE POETRY SERIES

1: Linda Anderson & Jo Shapcott (eds.)
Elizabeth Bishop: Poet of the Periphery

2: David Constantine: *A Living Language*
NEWCASTLE / BLOODAXE POETRY LECTURES

3: Julia Darling & Cynthia Fuller (eds.)
The Poetry Cure

4: Jo Shapcott: *The Transformers*
NEWCASTLE / BLOODAXE POETRY LECTURES
[Delayed title: now due 2012]

5: Carol Rumens: *Self into Song*
NEWCASTLE / BLOODAXE POETRY LECTURES

6: Desmond Graham: *Making Poems and Their Meanings*
NEWCASTLE / BLOODAXE POETRY LECTURES

7: Jane Hirshfield: *Hiddenness, Uncertainty, Surprise*
NEWCASTLE / BLOODAXE POETRY LECTURES

8: Ruth Padel: *Silent Letters of the Alphabet*
NEWCASTLE / BLOODAXE POETRY LECTURES

9: George Szirtes: *Fortinbras at the Fishhouses*
NEWCASTLE / BLOODAXE POETRY LECTURES

10: Fiona Sampson: *Music Lessons*
NEWCASTLE / BLOODAXE POETRY LECTURES

NEWCASTLE/BLOODAXE POETRY LECTURES

In this innovative series of public lectures at Newcastle University, leading contemporary poets speak about the craft and practice of poetry to audiences drawn from both the city and the university. The lectures are then published in book form by Bloodaxe, giving readers everywhere the opportunity to learn what the poets themselves think about their own subject.

NEWCASTLE/BLOODAXE POETRY SERIES: 10

FIONA SAMPSON

Music Lessons

Poetry and Musical Form

NEWCASTLE / BLOODAXE POETRY LECTURES

BLOODAXE BOOKS

Copyright © Fiona Sampson 2010, 2011

ISBN: 978 1 85224 909 0

First published 2011 by
Department of English Literary & Linguistic Studies,
Newcastle University,
Newcastle upon Tyne NE1 7RU,
in association with
Bloodaxe Books Ltd,
Highgreen,
Tarset,
Northumberland NE48 1RP.

www.bloodaxebooks.com
For further information about Bloodaxe titles
please visit our website or write to
the above address for a catalogue.

 Supported by
ARTS COUNCIL
ENGLAND

LEGAL NOTICE

All rights reserved. No part of this book may be
reproduced, stored in a retrieval system, or
transmitted in any form, or by any means, electronic,
mechanical, photocopying, recording or otherwise,
without prior written permission from Bloodaxe Books Ltd.

Requests to publish work from this book
must be sent to Bloodaxe Books Ltd.

Fiona Sampson has asserted her right under
Section 77 of the Copyright, Designs and Patents Act 1988
to be identified as the author of this work.

Cover design: Neil Astley & Pamela Robertson-Pearce.

Printed in Great Britain by
Bell & Bain Limited, Glasgow, Scotland.

Contents

Prelude   *7*

FIRST LECTURE
Point Counterpoint   *11*

SECOND LECTURE
Here is my space   *29*

THIRD LECTURE
How strange the change...   *46*

Coda   *61*

Notes   *63*

Acknowledgements

I'm very grateful to Bloodaxe Books, the English Department of Newcastle University and the Newcastle Centre for the Literary Arts for the opportunity to undertake these lectures. I would also like to thank the University of Warwick CAPITAL Centre, for a Fellowship which enabled me to start working on this topic, and John Kinsella, for his stimulating correspondence in response to early drafts.

i.m. Peter Porter
(1929-2010)

Prelude

In 1963, when the French composer Pierre Boulez decided to explore Western music as part of a radical return to fundamentals, he gave himself a warning that is also an alibi:

> – Any musician proposing to embark on an introspective analysis is always suspect.
> – Granted, reflection tends to be regarded in an ethereal light as "poetical" speculation, a safe position, after all…
> – …and it has the great advantage of thriving on imprecision and contenting itself with a few well-tried formulae. Vulgar technical considerations are not thought worthy of a place in the drawing room. They must remain modestly below stairs, and anyone choosing to stress them will certainly be considered ill-bred.[1]

I don't want to confine myself either to the drawing room or behind the green baize door. I'd prefer to imagine these lectures moving through spaces where readerly and writerly worlds meet: mediating, liminal spots rather like stairwells or landings. But Boulez is right: 'poetry' and 'music' are both risky terms, each freighted with symbolic resonance and expectation. Juxtapose them, and the risks double – since each form has to 'hear' the other as it is *in itself*, beyond metaphor, 'imprecision and […] formulae'. Yet it seems to me that this juxtaposition happens anyway: that all poetry *is* musical, in a 'vulgar technical' and absolutely un-'ethereal' sense, and that 'analysis' of the musical elements in poetry can therefore be both useful and suggestive.

Besides, this project also has a personal trajectory. My formation was musical: I left school at sixteen to enter the conservatoire system, of which my training had already made me a part. I was entirely uninterested in musicology: a performer whose obedience to my violinist "lineage" – that particular school of playing handed down from distinguished professor to pupil and which quickly leads back to Mitteleuropa or Odessa – was rewarded, as is customary, by scholarships and prizes. Something was transmitted to us within a *formal* discipline, in other words, which could not be transmitted without those enabling constraints. Yet, though it was highly sophisticated, this practice was also non-verbal. Proceeding by "feel" and "imitation", each of us moved towards what we believed to be the true identity of a piece, and made it our own. The "line" of an individual consciousness didn't commentate on this in words, but it did "play the tune in your head" as you played it through, working towards that Ideal version. Like all instrumentalists, I spent five or six hours every day throughout my teens and in my twenties *thinking without words.*

What does this have to do with poetry? Well, it establishes the empirical truth that such thinking is possible. We *can* have shaped, abstract, phrasal experiences prior to language. Also, since it's formed the way I am, it's formed my own thinking – about poetry in particular. Recently, for example, I've noticed that giving a reading feels just like giving a concert: the same process of *laying a form out through time* is carried out. I've also become aware of how much I compose by ear, rather than – say – numerology. I may count feet, or syllables, but a line must also have some phrasal momentum if it's to "work" for me. Finally, "coming out" about my first life as a musician has led to a series of collaborations with composers and performers. These experiences have combined to make me feel that the threshold between music and poetry, which the term *lyric* evokes, is wider, and more frequently trodden, than I'd thought.

They've also prompted the intuition that music occurs in poetry not only at the level of metre, and such strict forms as the ballad – through what we might call mimicry of musical repertory – leave alone in an ekphrastic topic, but as those deep forms like phrasal proportion which are prior to, yet carry and shape, language. These lectures are my first attempt to unpack that intuition: not as a special pleading for poet-musicians, nor even for a wider choice of musical contexts to our thinking in this area than just the three-minute chart lyric, but as a way to think about the movement and strength of poetic language in general.

They come, though, with a caveat of their own. It's more

than a quarter of a century since Paul de Man published his essay 'The Resistance to Theory'.[2] And though critical (read: post-structuralist) theory is just one intellectual fashion, existing culture's resistance to unfamiliar ways of thinking remains the context for thought experiment and intellectual adventure. Hearing deep form requires a particular kind of listening – sometimes, a shift of attention – which has the potential to make it seem as though trapdoors have opened right through what we conventionally think of as poetics. These lectures are not, however, resistant to any conventional forms of poetry, from iambic pentameter to Imagism. They aim to notice something additional to, rather than propose a critique of, those deep-seated disciplines. In other words, they simply ask the reader to listen differently.

A further legacy of life as a musician is the *discipline of interpretation*. I still feel the obligation to "get" a piece and its artistic strategies, however counterintuitive or far from my personal tastes they may be. Not understanding something is *my* failure: and the additional effort that failure spurs me to isn't a form of self-punishment, but basic professionalism. Knowing that the performer who can interpret Mozart with exemplary tenderness still fails if her Beethoven is leaden, it seems to me that a reader who can't "hear" George Herbert *because he doesn't write like*, say, John Donne fails in a similar way.

Since both Donne and Herbert have passed into the canon, that particular prejudice probably does little harm. But what happens when our competition-ridden climate makes readers feel that the *point* is to choose: to set up an opposition between, for example, the contrasted eco-mythologies of Alice Oswald and John Kinsella, or the alternatives Barry MacSweeney and W.S. Graham offer Northern Modernism after Basil Bunting? Overcoming the resistance to difference, or variety – especially to writing that feels challenging or unfamiliar – requires a *radical attention* to what's other: it brings us back to the importance of deep listening. This kind of listening might be simply a gesture of self-effacement, or lack of confidence; but it might also be a sign of poetic and intellectual acumen – as it is in, say, Frank Kermode's *Forms of Attention* or the poet Donald Revell's *The Art of Attention*.[3]

Shelley makes what turns out to be an analogous point in his *A Defence of Poetry*:

> The great secret of morals is love; or a going out of our own nature, and an identification of ourselves with [the beautiful that exists in] thought, action, or person, not our own. A man, to be greatly good, must imagine intensely and comprehensively; he must put himself in the place of another [...]. The great instrument of moral good is the imagination; and poetry administers to the effect by acting upon the cause. [...][4]

In other words, the capacity for attention might turn out to be central to poem-making. Music taught me to listen. I hope that, in listening to the musical element in verse, these lectures will find something useful about the nature of poetry itself.

FIRST LECTURE

Point Counterpoint

Line, however, is solely measure.
PAUL KLEE, 'On Modern Art'[1]

It seems something of a hostage to fortune – to put it another way, a cliché – to talk about poetry and music. We know that these practices are cousins and that, historically, the term *lyric* names this cousinship. As the *OED* says:

> Lyric: 1. Of or pertaining to the lyre; adapted to the lyre, meant to be sung; pertaining to or characteristic of song. Now used as the name for short poems (whether or not intended to be sung), usually divided into stanzas or strophes, and directly expressing the poet's own thoughts and sentiments. Hence, applied to the poet who composes such poems.[2]

The *Encyclopaedia Britannica* offers:

> Verse or poem that can, or supposedly can, be sung to musical accompaniment (in ancient times, usually a lyre) or that expresses intense personal emotion in a manner suggestive of a song.

Yet the actual form that music takes within poetry is contested and unclear. I think this matters on much more than simply a theoretical level. A great deal of the way we hear both our own and (alas) "rival" poetics, from pure pentameter to post-Beat free-form, is conditioned by assumptions about the nature of musicality in verse. Because these assumptions are unexamined, they have the power to strike false notes in our thinking. Besides, lyric cousinship implies that analogies exist between music and poetry. If that's the case, they're surely too useful to ignore. So I'd like to go looking for the lyric missing link. And I intend to start where music is often held to have started, with that *prima donna*, melody.

11

Igor Stravinsky's *Rite of Spring* opens with one of the most famous solos in the orchestral canon.[3] In fact, it starts with just one note, which has itself become instantly recognisable within the Western tradition: a single high E on the bassoon. The wind instrument's reedy, wooden timbre represents the wind, reeds and woods of the Russian *taiga*:

Like the *taiga*, that opening note seems as though it could go on forever (note the pause sign). Instead, it lapses into a figure that resembles a turn, one of those ornaments with which musicians traditionally italicise a note.[4] But the motif is repeated, and out of it arises an answering phrase. Next comes a tonal step sideways, as the clarinets contribute plangency. The bassoon repeats itself – there's an answering line from the cor anglais, in which an echo of hunting horns is probably no accident – and the instrumental chorus clusters round, baying and chattering.

Conveniently, this short passage illustrates all three of the musical characteristics I suspect can be found in poetry, and with which these lectures hope to deal. In 'How strange the change…' I look at chromaticism, play and the sensual "give" in language; tomorrow, I suggest that music's structural use of abstract form, including proportions such as the golden section, can also be seen in poetry. And today I want to look at the relationship between breath, line and phrase, and to suggest that this may be, or may produce, a fundamental measure of thought: and so of meaning.

Stravinsky's bassoon solo doesn't sound much like what we think of as tuneful. It doesn't try to charm, or offer the 'dying fall' of closure, and it isn't regular – arguably, that makes it harder to memorise. But this is just why it offers such a useful example of linear melody. For something fundamentally melodic does remain, willy-nilly: not beautifully modulated tonal *surface*, but something prior, and essential. The bassoon ventriloquises the human voice, and on a bad day it's even possible to detect Mr Punch's swazzle, or (*horreur*) a kazoo, in the double-reed bassoon's squawk. Yet the point here isn't the melody's sometimes stage-dummy *timbre*, but the way its singularity and its joined-up-ness combine to deliver what we recognise as a voice-trace.

But *how* do we recognise it? (It's no coincidence that, in Jacques Derrida's deconstruction of language, and hence thought, the *trace*, the 'mark of the absence of a presence', contains a puzzle about the actual nature of correspondence between *trace* and *what is traced*.)[5] We seem to make a connection between melody and what musicians do indeed call *line*: almost as if the air passing down the long, skinny bassoon were drawing a diagram of what we hear. The comparative anthropologist Tim Ingold's work on man-made lines, such as footpaths, or the warp of a carpet loom, underlines how these signify the connectedness, the 'and then... and then', of process. They aren't just evidence of a practice such as weaving; they are its *logic*.[6] In such traditional, collective *and so repeated* practices, the path is by definition always taken. The path is the desire line. By contrast, human activities which are *formed by specific choices* entail a phantom plurality, the 'paths not taken' of their discarded – or overlooked – alternatives. Think of a writer's notebook, or the shavings on a cabinet-maker's workshop floor. Composition, whether musical or poetic, works like this. Thus, Pierre Boulez quotes Henry Miller – 'What appears now before my eyes is the result of innumerable mistakes, withdrawals, erasures, hesitations; it is also the result of certitude' – to explain a 'logic of co-ordination' by which linear form, whether musical or literary, emerges from a multiplicity of experiments, drafts and aborted openings.[7]

This is one model of linearity: that of a singular conceptual succession. However melody, whether it's composed or traditional, also expresses a practical, internal logic all of its own. Melodic line is the 'and then... and then' of notes succeeding each other and, residually and often actually, the notes of a musical line are *also* connected by something internal, yet constitutive:

which is that they share a breath. Another way to say this is that melody can usually be sung – albeit sometimes only by a virtuoso specialist, a Jane Manning or a Christine Rice – and this singability is structural. It's even possible to sing the opening of the *Rite* (which has in any case been identified as transcribed folksong).[8] After all, the bassoonist too must connect those notes in a single breath.

So what *is* song? In 1947, that contested philosopher Martin Heidegger wrote that:

Singing and thinking are the stems neighbour to poetry.

They grow out of Being and reach into its truth.

Their relationship makes us think of what Hölderlin sings of the trees of the woods:

'And to each other they remain unknown,
So long as they stand, the neighbouring trunks.'[9]

I like the sense this gives of the *emergent* poem or song. As so often with Heidegger, not least thanks to his speculative etymology, there is a sense of origins. Which is to say a sense *both* of silence, the not-poem that comes before each particular poem; *and* of more general cultural origin.[10] We might also notice that song starts from silence because it starts with a preparatory in-breath; and this brings me to the intuition I'd like to explore next, which is that breath measures, and stages, the beginning, middle and end of *every* phrase, in language as in song. Thinking about this, I want to suggest, shifts us towards a richer understanding of "meaning": which I'll use the second part of this lecture to explore.

A song's first note has particular resonance because it emerges from silence to set the tonal scene within a generalised landscape of pitch and harmony. As a minimum, we find ourselves in a key or mode that includes this particular pitch. We hear who's singing. Rhythm and stress reveal this first note's role: is it an upbeat, that articulation and prolongation of the preparatory inhalation, or a key-note, stressed by the downbeat? Either way, it projects the song to come, throwing a formal template ahead of itself. (Without formal musical training we don't *know* that we know this – but our accultured ear does.) The significance of this first note is thus a legacy, within what we might call the song's consciousness, of the archaic gesture of utterance itself.

In fact, the preparatory in-breath is predicated by all oral forms. A poem also starts with a sense of anticipation, a prickle of pre-existence. At one level, of course, it's readers and audiences who bring this anticipatory sense to the completed poem, whether they come to a festival armed with knowledge of the poet's work or browse a volume in idle curiosity. But the lyric analogy also seems to suggest that it might be intrinsic.[11] For example, the classic Green Room advice is, *You aren't nervous, you're excited*. And some poets experience anticipation within the writing process in terms quite as bodily as any stage fright. Anne Stevenson calls this, 'That pregnant feeling! It's something like turning the circle on the top of the salt cellar until the salt comes out. You just have to get the holes matching'. Les Murray says, 'Poetry builds up in your mind like a charge. If you go in too early, you'll muck it up, if you go in too late, it'll be dry... At the right moment, the poem doesn't have words. It's a pressure.'[12] But it's the product as much as the process that makes this question of starting significant. Joseph Brodsky famously urged his students to cut any evidence of warming-up (that practice all too familiar to musicians: sure enough, pianist Alfred Brendel called his first collection of verse *Fingerzeig*). The finished poem should evoke the necessity of the always-already; it should appear as if it could never have taken any other form.

This is a specific poetics, of course. Brodsky's whole sense of poem-hood differs from today's North American poetry of process, written by figures like Jorie Graham or Brenda Hillman, whose varied antecedents include both D.H. Lawrence and Paul Celan.[13] In any case, the difficulty with this kind of negative definition is that it's not *necessarily* clear where the "real poem" of a poem starts. While such strategies are useful in the hands of a master of his own particular poetics, there *is* no formula – only good or bad judgement. Not every poet chooses to write like Brodsky, even whose longest poems – like *Gorbunov and Gorchakov*, or 'Lithuanian Nocturne' – start *in media res*.[14] Nor are the casual, hands-in-pocket openings of, say, the Robert Lowell of *For the Union Dead* the norm. 'Work-table, litter, books and standing lamp, / plain things [...]' ('Night Sweat') or 'It was a Maine lobster town – / each morning boatloads of hands / pushed off for granite / quarries on the islands' ('Water') are openings all right: they assert *here*, or *now*. They also get immediately to business, with no sense of throat-clearing. Yet many poets do clear their throats. Indeed, one solution to the instability of a poem's opening is to adopt the contrary strategy, and *fetishise* beginning. The traditional invocation of a muse – or its subversion, as in the famous opening of Rilke's first *Duino Elegy*: 'Who, if I cried out, would hear me then from the angel / ranks?' – is a gesture of demarcation, much like dimming the House lights or asking, 'Are you sitting comfortably?' Other first lines announce the programme: '*Arma virumque cano*', 'Yes, I remember Adlestrop'. Or they employ apostrophe: 'O wild West Wind, thou breath of autumn's being', 'Tiger! Tiger! [...]', 'Thou still unravished bride of quietness'. Even the contemporary orthodoxy that has a poem proceed *from* the concrete given towards affect or insight is really just another form of scene-setting:

> To the fishmonger's for a cod's head
> glistering like a pencil lead
>   (Jacob Polley, 'Crabbing') [15]

> By the headstones are toys and flowers and birds
> – budgies mainly, some owls –
> with wings that mill and whirr.
>   (Jamie McKendrick, 'By the Headstones') [16]

> It was the first gift he ever gave her,
> buying it for three francs in the Galeries
> in pre-war Paris.
>   (Eavan Boland, 'The Black Lace Fan My Mother Gave Me') [17]

However significant beginnings are, whenever something comes first something else – a middle – must come second. Arguably, breath reveals its scope more through the phrase-dependent *structuring* of a poem than in the opening gestures of *utterance*. Here, the *heldness* of breath or line comes to the fore. For E.M. Forster wasn't quite right when he suggested that 'the naked worm of time' is a purely narrative problem.[18]

'And then...and then' is also intrinsic to poetry: and not simply at the level of content but, more profoundly, at that of form. Unlike story, whose 'and then...and then' can be summarised, music and poetry both enact themselves sequentially. They are unparaphrasable; they can only be themselves *in going through* their own particular motions.[19]

This may be phenomenologically interesting, but what does it mean in poetic practice? Well, I suspect it implies a fundamental role for the line of breath. Working with adults with learning difficulties, I adopted the transparent strategy of writing down what they said, one phrase at a time. I recorded each new phrase as a new line. (This technique turned out to be much better suited to a poem like the one which follows, where the material was relatively difficult for its authors and so each phrase had been elicited by questions, than to work with a fluent speaker – for example, someone who's temporarily lost the ability to write after stroke – on a subject about which they've much to say. There, issues of selection have to intervene.)

I soon discovered that I wasn't indulging in anthropological eavesdropping. These were *dictated* lines of poetry, being composed by people who happened not to have literacy – or, often, advanced language skills. Here's a poem by the women of the St Cross Day Centre on the Isle of Wight:

The World Tree

Perhaps the world isn't a round ball.
Perhaps it's a tree.
The roots go down to the underworld
where anger and hate and criminals and murderers are,
and the branches go up to heaven
where God and the angels are.
That would mean that everything is joined
to everything else,
that the world is a place
where good and bad are joined.[20]

How can we tell this is a poem? One answer lies in its discursive role: its authors thought it was a poem and wanted it treated as such, and it performs many of the functions – condensation, record, heightening – a poem can undertake. But another answer is that, if you try to run its lines together as a paragraph, *you can still see the structure of the poem* in the balance of the phrases, their rhythmic similarity and their similarity of length and pitch:

> Perhaps the world isn't a round ball. Perhaps it's a tree. The roots go down to the underworld[,] where anger and hate and criminals and murderers are, and the branches go up to heaven[,] where God and the angels are. That would mean that everything is joined to everything else, that the world is a place where good and bad are joined.

This makes for flat, jerky writing. The poem is *not-prose*, because the equation between a line, or train, of thought and each line of the poem is structural. The *phrase* – it's no coincidence that this term's both linguistic and musical – delivers semantic and semiotic unity. Far from fragmenting or weakening the simple free verse form, a reinforcing layer-cake of poetic line, line of thought and melodic phrasal unit *creates* it. Indeed, arguably it's this coincidence that differentiates the lyric tradition, in its widest sense, from L=A=N=G=U=A=G=E poetry, or serial music. As well as the horizontal generation of surface, there is a vertical push-me-pull-you of relationship between the parts of speech, or pitch relations – which "inhabits" the language and makes it habitable by human meaning. 'The World Tree' may seem artless; but its 'roots go down' into the very way we use language.

Melody reminds us how fundamentally human the dimensions of such phrases are. When he starts to sing, breath maps a singer's body onto both pitch and words. The singer sings his own physical capacity – the volume of his lungs, the shape of his voice-box – out into the world. These sounds trace the workings of his body more purely than does speech, which is mediated by social inflection as well as by that stuttering effect of "thinking aloud" caused by the *psychological friction* of content on what's being said.[21] Yet what we call speech rhythms, the familiar shape of voiced units, do haunt the lines of every song, reproducing themselves through, and being reproduced by, breath-length. Breath entails both the possibility of, and a limit to, the spoken unit, which is therefore by necessity the basic unit of communication – of sense. A phrase *is* the length of a breath. And meaning-making mimics breathing: "what we can say" is both what we understand (take in) and what we have breath to say (expel). Tony Harrison's insistence that iambic pentameter is Yorkshire speech-rhythm may be a form of regional special pleading, but it usefully suggests how naturally metre can arise, with only the lightest top-and-tailing, from the spoken phrase.

Of course, the free verse of 'The World Tree' is a highly specific poetic. Phrase and line aren't necessarily identical in either free or formal verse. Free verse can enjamb with the best of them, while formal verse may seem defined by metre, its lineation entirely a question of footfall. The phrasal line offers two responses to this. One is that, nevertheless, there are several other poetries in which we can readily see phrasal lineation at work. The other is that apparently contrary examples reveal a deeper lyrical logic, in which the phrase is prior to and generates the poetic line it will then rest in or play against. That play will most often take the form of enlargement by enjambment, or of subdivision.

We readily think of Beat and Black Mountain poetics as predicated upon speech rhythms. But other, older prosodies also have the measure of the phrase. For example, it's the motor of parallelism, that two-phrase form so hugely influential on English prosody since the sixteenth century, when the Coverdale Psalter was incorporated into *The Book of Common Prayer*. At the opening of Psalm 27, parallelism operates in a variety of ways: to divide a verse (verse 3); to divide the verse and then *also act within* each half of the verse, thus making a doctrinal point – 'The Lord is the strength of my life' means the same as 'of whom then shall I be afraid?' (first verse); and to retain repetition within the half-verse but posit the reciprocity of question and answer (which make their own kind of parallel) at the half-verse point (verse 2):

> 1. The LORD is my light and my salvation; whom then shall I fear? The LORD is the strength of my life; of whom then shall I be afraid?
>
> 2. One thing have I desired of the LORD, which I will require, Even that I may dwell in the house of the LORD all the days of my life, to behold the fair beauty of the LORD, and to visit his temple.

3. For in the time of trouble he shall hide me in his tabernacle; Yea, in the secret place of his dwelling shall he hide me, and set me up upon a rock of stone.[22]

Among the earliest English verse to be influenced by this Hebrew form – besides the hendiadys so prevalent in Shakespearean dialogue – were the freshly-composed antiphons of *Common Prayer* itself:

Priest O Lord, open thou our lips
Answer And our mouths shall show forth thy praise.
Priest O God, make speed to save us
Answer O Lord, make haste to help us.
 (from *Matins*)

Repetitive rather than dialectical, the to-and-fro of versicle and response owes less to Platonic dialogue than to a sense of *rhythmic entailment*, that what-goes-up-must-come-down feeling which the regularity of a formal metrical line also produces. All the same, just as in Socratic dialectic, its one-step-at-a-time oscillation between approach and standstill leads the mind to *something beyond* itself.

Liturgy doubtless intends that to be God. Yet it's the singing human who is posited by every breath, and so at the limit of every phrase. Of plainchant, that liturgical equivalent predating Anglicanism, Olivier Messiaen notes that:

'the ordering of movement' [...] involves the alternation of rises and falls that the Greeks so aptly called *arses* and *theses*. Now, all well-written music contains this constant alternation. Plainchant, to cite only one case, is an uninterrupted succession of *arses* and *theses*, elevations and drops, rises and falls, as was perfectly delineated by the greatest theoretician of plainchant, Dom Mocquereau.[23]

These counter-balanced exchanges demonstrate the extent of a phrase: how after a certain point – a sort of phrasal life expectancy – it topples over into the next. Crucially for the intrinsic 'and then...and then' of poetry, that reveals how a phrase precipitates a posterity: a *what next*? If there *is* no next phrase, the *next* into which we're led is the silence that lurks, like a tricky manoeuvre, at the end of each phrase. Silence seems particularly close at line-ends, whose natural porosity allows it to leak into a poem. Sometimes it produces the pleasurable prolongation of enjambment, like Edward Thomas's casual trick of timing that gives us his pause – 'No one left and no one came / On the bare platform' – in 'Adlestrop'; but at others it generates a vertiginous *aporia* after which the next line must virtually re-start the poem. It would be easy to think of this silence as a kind of ghost- or anti-poem, with the potential to undo or overwhelm language. Small wonder, then, that poems tend to *end* as if pre-empting the risk of dissolution.

Some gestures of completion are pre-eminently semantic. Douglas Dunn, for example, has a tendency to the kind of summing-up which is also a summoning-up of poetic forces. Think of the so-quotable end of 'A Removal from Terry Street': 'That man, I wish him well. I wish him grass.' (Dunn's naval verse-novel *The Donkey's Ears* ends with a terrifying bull's-eye on the very last word, 'dressed to meet the horrid sea.')[24] Strong endings can also be aurally seductive. End-rhyme is, arguably, no more compelling than internal rhyme: both establish coherence, with all this suggests of control, authority and necessity, not to mention an existential Order of Things. But end-rhyme also locks the lyric shut. Think of Philip Larkin, that master of the punch-line: 'Begin afresh, afresh, afresh', '[…] somewhere becoming rain', 'Unlucky charms, perhaps.'[25] His much-quoted 'What will survive of us is love' clinches, even as it undermines, a (slant) rhyme ('prove/love') which tracks straight back to Marlowe's 'Passionate Shepherd':

> […] The stone fidelity
> They hardly meant has come to be
> Their final blazon, and to prove
> Our almost-instinct almost true:
> What will survive of us is love.
> ('An Arundel Tomb')[26]

Rhyme locks this stable-door *before* the horse can bolt: and the bolts are, perhaps, drawn all the tighter because of the instability ('they *hardly* meant […] *almost*-instinct *almost* true') of the poem's triply-qualified conclusion.

However, it's here that – to mix a metaphor – we come up against that elephant in the music room which these lectures plan to squeeze past. Metre, rhyme's "handmaid", is a principle of organisation that verse and music (whether in traditional or free forms) have so clearly in common that we tend to fall back on it when we want to think about the musical element in poetry. Metre promotes our heart over our lungs as the fundamental of poetic music: it reminds us how language moves, like a pulse, between stressed and unstressed sounds. But I want to skirt round this topic for three reasons. The first is that, quite simply, metre is a central and already much-discussed element of both poetry and thinking about poetry: formalist Anne Stevenson, for example, says, 'You can't get around the fact that a rhythmic pattern of stresses AND of long and short intonations (notes), AND of alliterative consonants plus assonantal vowels determine the "tune" of all the best poems in the English language.'[27] However central *using* it may be within the experience of writing and reading, though, engaging here with this capacious, familiar topic will just restate what's obvious, leaving little room for less familiar material.

Secondly though, I think we should be careful about hearing the heartbeat, important though it undoubtedly is, as *the* musical fundamental.[28] Music itself suggests otherwise. While much of the Western tradition, from 'The Ode to Joy' to Trance tracks by way of 'Tam Lin' and reggae, is indeed built foursquare on simple time, there's also the regular compound, three time, that powers so many traditional tunes: waltz, jig and shuffle alike. And we shouldn't forget the seven-time (*one-two one-two one-two-three*) of the Balkan *kolo*, where the extra beat is what powers the rhythm along, just as the extra "step" in an alexandrine keeps readers on their toes. Its push-me-pull-you – not syncopation but something that literally wrong-foots the tune – shows up the provincial logic of Eliot's peasants 'Lifting heavy feet in clumsy shoes' in their two-by-two stamping trochees. Moreover, Arabic and Indian forms demonstrate how a line of musical thought can *master* metrical structure. When a *raga* or *samā* takes a line for a walk the ear *follows* the music as it moves through and extends harmonic and rhythmic possibilities. We need to think beyond as well as through local national ways of writing if we're thinking about the nature of poetry in itself:

and that breath can incorporate *all* these metrical forms seems convincingly to suggest its role is more fundamental than that of pulse.

But does breath itself have shape as well as length? I suspect it does, and that this is what we hear in the "common-lore" of *grammatical music*, when we can follow the shape of a conversation in a language we don't know, or despite the muffling bedroom wall. In that strange experience of understanding without understanding, we glimpse the shape of the phrase *itself*: a set of speech-forms or relationships *prior* to particular vocabulary. Perhaps this isn't surprising. Since breath is the medium of speech, it makes sense to think of speech as having had to evolve *within* that breath: something that's most noticeable when it breaks down. Think of how children run out of breath and snatch another in the middle of a phrase when they're reporting a message or reading aloud. Or how prose dreamt up entirely on the page or in the head – whether legalese or obsessive-compulsive graphomania – forms an indigestible linguistic bolus. My third reason for avoiding discussion of metre, then, is that I'm interested in those aspects of musical form that I believe *underlie*, complement and enable, metre.

In other words, I suspect we can go on to speculate that, in generating and limiting the melodic unit, breath may outline, or measure, the *semantic* unit too. Like any marriage of the musical and the semantic, this possibility would be of vital interest to poetry. It's small wonder that Mandelstam's idea of 'composing on the lips' is so attractive to a poet like John Burnside, whose extended lyrics employ an elastic linearity to join idea to idea and image to image.[29] The phrasal unit plays an equally *propulsive* role in such sharply contrasted poetics as those of C.K. Williams or of Jorie Graham, each of whom uses repeated *phrasal initiatives* to build long, urgent lines:

> I have talked too much. Have hurried. Have tried to cover the fear
> with curiosity. Also amazement. It is fear. Also know that a poem
> is, in the end, not supposed to scare you, sweet friend, reader,
> I believe you to be a person who would hide me if it came to that.
> Wouldn't you? Whoever I am or happen to be.
>
> (Posterity)[30]

However, behind the satisfyingly integrative idea that breath is a *measure* of meaning lurks another, even more suggestive: that *melody is itself* semantic. In other words, it's not just that we hear the *phrasal unity* of whatever can be said before the breath runs out; but that such rhythmic, meaningful units have an aural character of their own – a *meaningful melody*, a 'song without words'. But thinking about this means thinking about the nature of meaning itself; to do that I'm going to resort to lyric common ground.

My sense is that one of the reasons contemporary philosophers of music, like Peter Kivy, run into difficulties when they think about the possibility that a musical phrase has a denotative grammar is that they assume that whatever's *semantic* must be *narrative*.[31] But, even if meaning is only whatever can be done by language – even if we use 'meaning' in this narrow sense – poetry, along with other familiar forms such as the shopping list, or Rules and Regulations, offers another model than simple story-telling. For example, the meaning of a poem might be the feeling or atmosphere it *evokes*.[32] Moreover, poetic language doesn't exclusively point to something beyond itself. It can also gesture *to* itself: in rhyme or "purple" passages (we might think of these signalling "poetic importance"), or by deploying a form, such as the ghazal, with a particular set of literary-historical resonances. So at least one meaning of a poem could be "the way it tells it", that particularity of *these* words in *this* order which, apparently, gets lost in translation. If we return to the musical half of the lyric analogy, we can also see that meaning is quite simply whatever is not *meaningless*, or (in both its popular and conventional meanings) *random*. For if meaning were always something external that music had to point out or mimic, abstract music – everything purely instrumental, apart from progamme music – would be "meaningless". Yet that's not our experience. We experience it as meaning*ful* – even when it's *not* evoking a particular emotion: as non-arbitrary, but cohering in a recognisable form. Music makes meaning *in its own terms*: its meaning is *musical*.

So both sides of the lyric analogy suggest that melody can be meaningful in itself. And this in turn implies that the line of a phrase might be able to generate meaning even *prior to the words* it carries: think of the downward turn of closure, or staccato repetition. This would mean that musical form could entail the textual, rather than necessarily the other way around. That turns out to be a working assumption in ethnomusicology. For example, in the 1970s János Maróthy was able to reconstruct how "variative" song – a single, unmetrical musical phrase repeated with variation – was used in European tribal society for the recitation of epics, and its further occurrence in metrical, strophic form was evidence that in more recent, feudal times epic was translated into ballad.

But there are many other examples of musical meaning producing, or reproducing, the semantic. The choric strophe and antistrophe choreographed both the narrative movement of Greek drama and the on-stage movements of the chorus. Elsewhere, post-classical music often sets texts without reference to traditional metre; yet these non-arbitrary settings identify non-metrical, semantic stresses and releases within the language. One of the pieces Benjamin Britten sets in his *Serenade for Tenor, Horn and Strings* is Tennyson's 'The Splendour Falls'. The opening couplet is not Lord Alfred's finest hour: 'The splendour falls on castle walls / And snowy summits old in glory.' You don't have to be a student of Hopkins to hear the depressive effect of vowelling-on from the *e-our* of splendour down to the *a-e* of castle and the *o*s that dominate the second line. The tangle of abstraction ('old in glory') isn't exactly vivid. But Britten lifts up the Es of 'splen-' and 'tle' towards a glowing 'old' as he explodes this phrase from its metrical box.

In this example, music seems *illustrative* of what the text is doing. In effect, it's ekphrastic. (One useful side-effect of thinking about setting in this way – as something carried out *alongside* the poem rather attempting to in some way complete it – is that it solves the problem of why one should set poetry to music when it already has its own musicality. Phrased slightly differently this becomes another question: Why illustrate a poem? Clearly *The Lindisfarne Gospels*, for example, weren't produced in the belief that the Biblical texts were incomplete and needed help. So the answer to both puzzles is surely that oldest one in the creative book: *because you can*.)

However, if we think of such settings not simply as illustration but as a speech act, we shift the stakes for *melodic* meaning to denotation. When the celebrant of a rite lifts his voice from spoken word into chant, he performs a speech-act concerned with heightening, highlighting, or demarcating the occult in discourse. There are also traces of melody as speech act in our consensual use of pitch. We all know what Shakespeare means by 'that phrase again, it had a dying fall' when Duke Orsino wallows in lover's melancholy: I know of no culture in which an upward flourish is a gesture of *tristesse*. Nor is it coincidence that house and car alarms appropriate the dolorous descending minor third of children's calls: *Coming, Coo-ee, Mummee*.

Melody and speech act reconverge in the human tendency to put words to tunes. When bored musicians, or football fans, improvise obscenity to fit anything from Tchaikovsky's Fifth Symphony to *Jesus Christ Superstar*, it feels as if these *a posteriori* lyrics have been implied or even generated by the music; as if melody can generate meaning in ways somewhat akin to grammar. Think of Frederick Chopin's *Prelude* Op 28 n 20, set by Barry Manilow as 'Could It Be Magic' (1975); the first movement of Haydn's *Emperor Josef Quartet* Op 76 n 3 later becoming the German National Anthem.[33] When grammar and melody move towards such coincidence, they seem to do so through the phrasal logic of a breath: its rise and fall, and its deployable extent. Charles Olson's famous 1950 essay, 'Projective Verse', identifies the poem's movement – a kind of breath of life – with human breath, which he sees as a *generative* principle:

> I say a projective poet will [go] down through the workings of his own throat to that place where breath comes from, where breath has its beginnings, where drama has come from, where, the coincidence is, all act springs.

Problematically, the essay goes on to conflate this universal principle with a personal poetics:

> [...] ONE PERCEPTION MUST IMMEDIATELY AND DIR-ECTLY LEAD TO A FURTHER PERCEPTION. [...] Get on with it, keep moving, keep in, speed, the nerves, their speed, the perceptions, theirs, the acts, the split second acts, the whole busi-

ness, keep it moving as fast as you can, citizen. And if you also set up as a poet, USE USE USE the process at all points, in any given poem always, always one perception must must must MOVE, INSTANTER, ON ANOTHER![34]

Olson's special-case argumentation misses the point that the line in a poem – that musical semantic unit – is *always* based on breath. Composing 'on the breath' is simply composition carried out by a living human (so that's everything, then, except what's computer-generated). Within the continuity of human being and thought, one thing *always* follows another. Breath is, in other words, an *impersonal* principle, rather like the old imperial measure of a foot, which doesn't correspond to a particular shoe-size but indicates human scale in general. The phrasal line of breath in a poem isn't a record of Olson's personal lung-capacity, but of human breath in general. As the old lyrical-musical use of that term implies, it is a "measure" of, roughly speaking, "what we can say".

Like no other form, a poem's lineation records this human grammar, and takes from it its own characteristic "music". The breath-formed phrase attests to the human scale, or voicedness, of this form which pays *particular* attention to it. But, as we've seen, poetry also does this in at least four further ways: by incorporating such aspects of performativity as stylised beginnings and ends (which resist silence); through allowing phrasal music to generate the poem; and by its deployment of the musical character of grammatical units and of the meaningfulness of the musical elements in language. Dada, for example, heard these originary musical elements as occurring at the level of syllables, and advocated a poetry led by them:

> I want my own stuff, my own rhythm, and vowels and consonants too, matching the rhythm and all my own. [...] I let the vowels fool around. I let the vowels quite simply occur, as a cat meows... Words emerge, shoulders of words, legs, arms, hands of words. Au, oi, uh. One shouldn't let too many words out. A line of poetry is a chance to get rid of all the filth that clings to this accursed language, as if put there by stockbrokers' hands, hands worn smooth by coins.[35]

Poems utter themselves one line at a time. Perhaps this is so that they can be clearly heard. Or maybe it's because linearity is the only real sense that can be made of our sequential lives: think of the 'and... and' of a Abbas Kiarostami movie, or the way a child tells what happened in school today. As the White Knight said to Alice, 'You start at the beginning and go on to the end.'[36] Maybe poetry's understanding of the power of enactment is so strong – as in the aboriginal Australian song-lines, those journeys that, to simplify, tell the world into being – that it has to *adopt* linear "life-forms". Or perhaps unity brings a rare experience of resolution to the multiplicity of experience. (Exceptions I can think of include verses with contrapuntal settings, or the "wall of sound" created by experimentalists like French sound poet Patrick Dubost.)

These are speculations. What we *do* know is that the line of breath is inflected and flexible: it's something living and human. It is not a carapace. It's not like the shoes of the canonical greats, which challenge us to fill them exactly or fail. Breath slips through the cracks in the metrical pavement. Yet it remains exact and elective. Far from the kind of careless reading, or writing, which the term "voice" sometimes implies, breath is an *additional* connector, a *further* logic, underpinning metre and form. Breath, it *transpires*, is not only the human measure within language, but its animator – giving musical sense to semantic content, and ensuring a grammar for sound.

SECOND LECTURE

Here is my space

*An angel with no face embraced me
and whispered through my whole body:
'Don't be ashamed of being human, be proud!
Inside you vault opens behind vault endlessly.
You will never be complete, that's how it's meant to be.'*

TOMAS TRANSTRÖMER, 'Romanesque Arches',
tr. Robin Fulton [1]

When Mark Antony says, at the opening of *Antony and Cleopatra*, 'Let Rome in Tiber melt, and the wide arch / Of the ranged empire fall! Here is my space', he demarcates the play's wider concern with personal/public distinctions quite as much as he declares his love for Cleopatra. And today I want to explore the possibility that, whatever poetry *seems* to be telling us – by way of narrative, or through "confessing" emotion – it's also enacting an abstract, formal process. My suspicion is that such pure, or prior, abstract form is one of the most important things poetry shares with music. In fact I suspect it's where both the language-as-art paradox, and its resolution, are located. While every other art-form can resort to pure abstract form, language seems to be led by the opposing principle of denotation. Yet in practice we accept that poetry is an art-form; we even seem to assume it makes room for, or performs, some discursive gesture beyond simple reportage.

This is conceptually tricky territory. After all, poetic form, from villanelle to free verse, is amply mapped; and the affinities between strict forms, dance-music and metrical song are obvious.

Yet I can't help being interested in the forms that *underlie* (in the senses both of differing from and of generating) poetics, operating at that abstract, structural level where thematic building-blocks are juxtaposed, or a poem changes momentum because it's nearing its conclusion. (I'm aware I need to use the loaded term "structural" carefully, after Ferdinand Saussure and Vladimir Propp, in this context charged with both linguistics and ethnology.)

Yesterday, thinking about breath showed us the poetic line as a measure of the embodied, universal human; while thinking about the line led to the idea that, even without words, it's a *unit* of sense – and thus, part of *getting the measure of* the world *in which* we're embodied. Both ideas remind me of those famous Leonardo da Vinci drawings that "prove" various proportions against his image of a man. This isn't, perhaps, surprising: the search for intrinsic truths that could stabilise the chaos of abstraction has been a continuing human theme. We look for form and pattern in order to make sense of experience. But as part of that search we also have to ask ourselves whether we *discover* or to *devise* such forms. What's *true*, rather than *conceptually possible*? Is the Higgs Boson particle a fact, or a conceptual lever? And if it's true in some special way, "true in maths" as it were, does that mean other things can also be "true in thought": fictional characters, for example? On the other hand, geometry does work both as a closed conceptual system and empirically: I really do need that number of tiles to finish the bathroom wall. Still more confusingly, when patterns do occur in nature, which might be one definition of "truth", they tend not quite to add up. Musicians deal with this anomaly routinely, in the problem of equal temperament; which makes it a useful starting point for any thinking about pure form.

Quickly to recap: pitch appears to be a *given*, since certain relationships between the notes of the harmonic series – octaves, fifths, thirds, all the apparatus of a Western key – are correlated by overtones. If you sound both notes of an interval perfectly in tune together, the next note "up" the series will sound itself. This feels like God, or the universe, giving you a tick: but it's simply the result of the way each pitch pulses at a particular frequency per second, which is therefore related to the frequency of every other pitch. Especially strong relationships – frequency ratios of 1:2, 2:3 or 3:4 – constitute the harmonic series.[2] However, although pitch continues to repeat each key to an infinity of both higher and lower notes on either side of what a musician plays, and out beyond the range of the human ear, the extreme verity which produces overtones is only *local*. If you pitch several consecutive intervals perfectly, the outer notes of that series will no longer be in tune with each other. (Pythagoras was the first to understand that a *diatonic comma* is necessary between twelve consecutive perfect fifths and seven perfect octaves, because this Cycle of Fifths doesn't quite add up. B# is *not* exactly C, in the conjuring trick beloved of music teachers. Musicians call this non-identicality, which sounds like out-of-tuneness, an *enharmonic* change; and they locate it particularly around the accidentals, between for example F# and G♭.)[3]

Musicians have always adjusted to these natural facts. Within a key, most decent fiddle-players flatten their sub-mediants and heighten their leading notes just as, in the wider realm of absolute pitch, they sharpen their F#s and flatten their G♭s. These notes are customarily treated as synonyms though in fact, just as there *is* no such thing as a synonym – since each alternative offers a variant meaning, resonance and register as well as sound – the hyperactive brightness of F# is *not* identical with the pitch-pine gloom of G♭. The key-character of perfect pitch makes it impossible *fully* to transpose musical material. (A gleefully exaggerated analogy might be the false synonyms of Les Murray's 'Employment for the Castes in Abeyance', where a translation machine renders 'out of sight, out of mind' as 'invisible lunatic'.)[1] However in the Baroque era the rise in importance of keyboard instruments, with their wide range of pre-tuned notes, meant such differentiations were lost. The ringing endorsement of absolute pitch was smoothed away by a diplomatic compromise that preserved the *form* of harmonic relations, but not quite their content. Famously, J.S. Bach's *Well-Tempered Klavier* (1722) was written to demonstrate the possibilities this strategy opened up: possibilities since further enlarged by the development of equal temperament.[5]

Bach's 'Forty Eight' Preludes and Fugues showcase a dialectic between radical adventurism and profound conservatism, which we could say arises from the human search for existential pattern. Deep foundations enable extravagant superstructures, and to this religious composer whatever was given was not accidental but *God*-given. This meant not only that music had certain inalienable qualities, such as harmonic relationships, but that it *should reflect and celebrate* their evidence of Divine Order by exploring and exploiting what such harmonies could do. Harmonic form was not only a *means* of music, but an *end*. Over twenty centuries earlier, Pythagoras had posited another, similarly totalising, metaphysics in which the mathematical coherence of the musical cycle of fifths predicated an entire music of the spheres.[6] He reasoned that the moving planets sound a note according to their place along a heavenly monochord stretching from pure spirit to pure matter. This seems less purely speculative when we remember that, for Pythagoras, number characterised the entire universe, from colour spectrum to gender relations. Besides, as if to suggest they might after all be key to the Order of Things, these same number relations do occur in a range of physical contexts. For example, in the nineteenth century John A. Newlands discovered the *law of octaves* which, though it turns out to be one of those imperfectly-occurring natural patterns, gave the Periodic Table its name. In his formulation, 'When elements are arranged in increasing order of their atomic mass, [every] eighth element resembles the first in physical and chemical properties just like the eighth note on a musical scale resembles the first note.'[7]

But even if these abstract, mathematical forms *are* all around us, and regulate and generate harmonic structures, can they be used by *poetry* in distinctive, purposeful ways? I want to argue that they can, and that abstract form – that is, form determined in relation to itself rather than by expressive or meaning-led considerations – occurs in poetry in at least three ways. I'd like to suggest that we can see it at work in *density*, in *impersonality*, and in a *temporal architecture* – non-random, abstract form structured by time rather than space – common to music and poetry. I'll think about each of these in turn – and ask whether such formal qualities, where they do appear in poems, are or could be *intentional*. If so, the abstract ratios and patterns of mathematical harmony may turn out to be among the most musical elements of poetics.

What could *density* mean, in this context? We might begin at the beginning, like any music student, by addressing Bach's chorales. Apparently metrically unadventurous, and characterised by heftily columnar progressions, these short hymn-like pieces – some sung, some instrumental – can sound undemonstrative, even impenetrable. Their texts draw the kinds of general conclusions ('Thy will be done', 'In Thee we trust') which can only be filled with meaning by the particular, personal process – for example, a struggle to understand or to be reconciled – involved in *getting to the Amen*. It's as if there can be no spiritual shortcuts and, were the rehearsal room door to swing open for a moment, or the radio briefly to tune past, we'd hear an isolate chord, but 'miss the meaning'. While the chorales perform a series of in-fact-astonishing tensions and syntheses, we have to follow or sing *through* these progressions in order to hear them. In *Christ lag in Todesbanden*, BWV 4, an Easter chorale on Luther's words which is also the basis of a cantata, the ambivalence with which the Christian contemplates Good Friday – Christ, crucified and 'lying bound by death', is not yet resurrected – is tellingly portrayed by the oscillation between major and minor. Only faith, at this stage, can secure the closing (major) *tierce de Picardie*: see score overleaf.

In this example, prayer is the process that must be gone through. But so must every form of thought (poetry not excepted), for as Jonathan Miller has said, 'Language is successive'.[8] Nevertheless, Bach's performance of the individual struggle with "God questions" does have particular analogies with the very varied poetries that attempt something similar: from George Herbert's and Thomas Traherne's, to Herbert Lomas's *Letters in the Dark* or Donald Hall's struggle to come to terms with the death of his wife Jane Kenyon, in *The Painted Bed*. Even more closely-analogous is the *horizontal harmonic strategy*, or

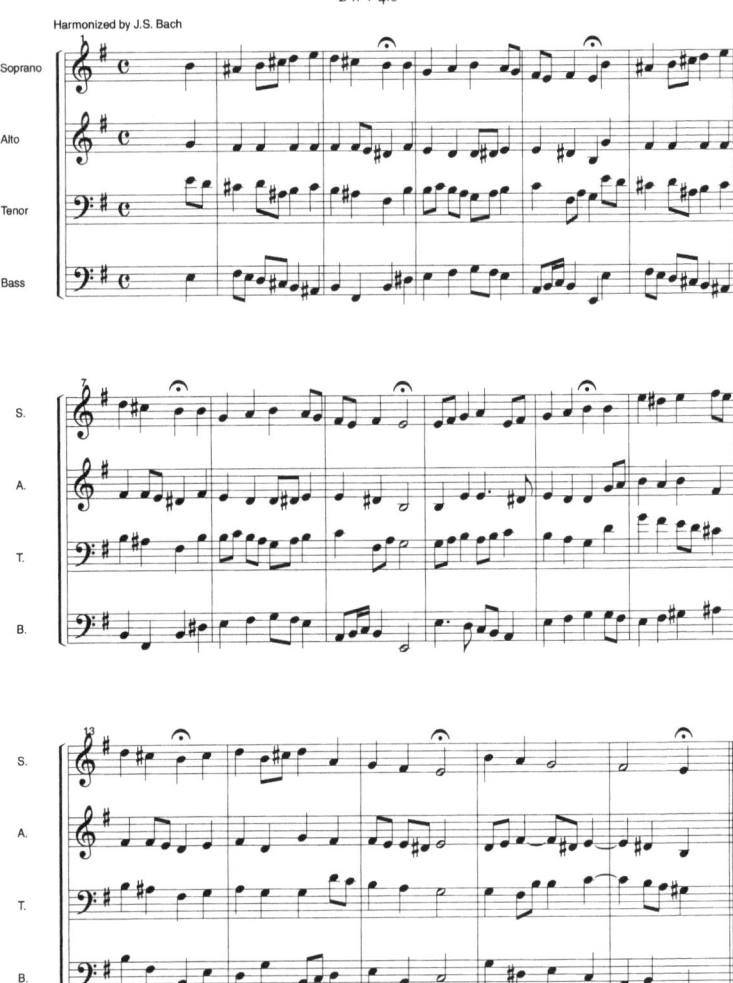

tonal exchange, that appears in Gerard Manley Hopkins's 'Terrible Sonnets'. In 'Carrion Comfort' a word-order that wrenches itself away from convention doesn't interrupt, but intensifies, lament:

> Not, I'll not, carrion comfort, Despair, not feast on thee;
> Nor untwist – slack they may be – these last strands of man
> In me ór, most weary, cry *I can no more*. I can;
> Can something, hope, wish day come, not choose not to be.[9]

The three *nots* of this first line, passing through a double negative *and beyond*, include the very first word, which refuses the conventional 'No – ' and by that refusal amplifies itself, its *ot* catching and tangling with 'carrion com*fort*'. Reprised in the fourth line, however, these *nots* settle back to a double negative – that resists suicide in the barest of terms. Among the many other sensations crammed into these rhymed, seven-stressed lines are repeated lips-shut *m*s and exclamatory zero *o*s, which don't just mimic sudden speechlessness ('shock and awe'), but repeatedly open and shut the vowel-music of the poem, so that we experience each word – and realisation – as *gained from* whatever came before it: silence, incomprehension, or the absence of God.

Musicians, like poets, understand that scrunches of intensity, whether forming such a trajectory or isolated as "hits", are part of what we might call the vertical meaning of a work. They're depth-charges, operating in the same way as poetry's polymorphous perversity – from, say, the *double entendre* of Robin Robertson's boozy whore who 'drank [him] under the table' to the Metaphysical sting in George Herbert's 'Love' – or its formal concentration.[10] (A ready example of this is the concentrated final couplet of William Shakespeare's 'Sonnet 18' – 'So long as men can breathe, or eyes can see, / So long lives this, and this gives life to thee'[11] – which is definitive in both senses at once. The masculine-ending 'see'/'thee' rhyme seems to "speak over" those arguably-feminine values 'lives'/'gives', and retrospectively appropriates all the corroborative *l*-alliterations, as if masculinity were a winner-takes-all button.)

But the closest poetic equivalent to Bach's chorales may be that found in Emily Dickinson's signature tension between undemanding grammatical structure and sophisticated metaphysical idea:

> I cannot dance opon my toes –
> No Man instructed me –
> But oftentimes, among my mind,
> A glee possesseth me [12]

The hymnal metre, plain as Shaker weatherboarding, is conspicuous for its constraint, and this intensifies the subversive shock of double meanings. For Dickinson's 'Man' is just as much individual masculine suitor as he is the possibility of the divine, defined in opposition to mere humanity. And listen to how the metre lifts the very first foot into contention – opposing 'I can' to 'No Man' with nice immodesty – and highlighting, thus, the paradoxical, metrical ghost of 'I can' within 'I *can*not'. These apparently meek, obedient iambs are in fact anything but: the poet does indeed 'dance', at least 'among [her] mind'. In the rest of this poem's relatively expansive five stanzas she lists dance-figures, and enjambs across both line- and stanza-break.

Dickinson's virtuoso play with metrical conservatism suggests what I'd like to call *a rule of poetic density*: a principle according to which, the more complex a poem's ideas are, the less baroque its versification may be. It somehow seems as if there's only so much material, or attention, a poem can sustain before it collapses into jingle, rant, prose-poem, polemic or memoir. If combined with expansive versification, highly ambitious thought places poetry under strain. I'm thinking of the risk of hubris in Ezra Pound's *Pisan Cantos*; or the way even a master like Geoffrey Hill, in attempting to bring the sensibility of the King James Bible to bear on the State of the Nation in *Canaan* and other late collections, places his own diction under such pressure that it moves out of reach of many readers.

Doubtless, if I were a Pythagorean, I'd reduce this to an equation, say D=CV (density = content x versification). But poetry proceeds by example. From among the expansive versifiers, Beat poets' sustained riffs are notorious. A capacious poem like Allen Ginsberg's 'America' is a variety act that brings together multivalent elements, from food politics to queer theory. Yet its self-conscious compendiousness in fact produces what in *formal* terms is pretty much a simple list poem. Elsewhere, the Anglophone verse-novel, enjoying a revival since the 1990s, applies the easily-assimilated motor of narrative to the heft of extended verse. Nothing interrupts the momentum of its singular trajectory, perhaps best exemplified by Derek Walcott's *Omeros* – terza rima in iambic sestrameter – or Vikram Seth's George Meredith-inspired sonnets in *Golden*

Gate. Like Les Murray's *Fredy Neptune*, with its two hundred and fifty-two pages of octets, these volumes *keep metrical step*. Compare the fate of four comparatively-recent verse novels: the easy-reading successes of John Haynes's *Letter to Patience* and Adam Foulds's *The Broken Word* contrast with the degree to which Glyn Maxwell's multi-narrator *The Sugar Mile*, a symbolic and transformative book which put 9/11 in the context of the Blitz – or Ciaran Carson's exquisite, palindromic *For All We Know* – have been overlooked.

On the other side of the density balance, complex metaphysical poetry seems to thrive in tight form. As Hopkins demonstrated, sonnet's tangy paradox and Janus-faced extended metaphors are suggestive not only of complexity but of the dual nature of meta/physical experience. But the form is also discrete, predictable and short. Moreover, this isn't to suggest the Death of God in an era of free verse. R.S. Thomas's late great poems of faith use a tightly reined-in free form whose skeletal diction, short lines and emotive register slow and focus the reading eye. 'Le Dormeur du Val' opens, 'In the beginning / the word. Will the word / be at the end?'[13] Pauline Stainer's hair's-breadth perfection produces such clarity that her meditations on such unfashionable topics as incarnation can be read and understood even by a largely-secular contemporary audience:

Madonna lilies

Their fluted whites
should rebuke all fever

but they thirst, they thirst,
tongues urgent as pollen

for the angel's transaction,
the accidents of bread and wine.[14]

Of course, this notional "rule of density" is just a device, more thought experiment than technical principle, to be dismantled once its work is done. But it does hint that there might be poetic structures that don't depend upon, but instead *produce*, the conventions of versification. What, then, of *impersonality* in verse?

Yesterday breath emerged as a *human* principle, yet also as an *impersonal* measure underpinning the melodic and poetic line. But music seems to demonstrate that impersonality could be the whole *basis* of form. As we've seen, it's intrinsically non-denotative in the narrative or realist sense (to a greater degree even than dance, where the human body figures at the level of representation and through gestures of which some are also part of everyday action and communication). But, not being random or accidental, it must speak to *something*: it must, at least, be organised in terms of its own nature. That organisation is, thus, both non-denotative and substantive: in other words, abstract and formal. Its terms are self-generated and in a way, hermetic. However, since language *is* denotative, poetry's relationship with pure form seems *prima facie* more complicated than music's. Yesterday I explored the possibility of non-denotative organisation (meaning) in both music and grammar as a solution to this conundrum. Today, instead of moving music *towards* this kind of meaning, I want to shift language *away* from it by looking at how poems *work themselves out*, impersonally and independently, as form alone (in ways we're used to thinking of a piece of music as doing).

I suggest this is pretty much what happens whenever a poet reads on automatic pilot. It's a familiar enough scenario: you're tired, the train was late, you had to rush to the venue. And now, you don't quite know how, you're on stage and halfway through an old standby. You give the thing its usual shape – the pauses and intonation – but you just aren't quite *there*. The poem has a voice, but it's not *your* voice. Instead, you find yourself putting the form of the poem *out there* as a sequence of phrasal gestures and timings. And this both feels, and does not feel, somehow fraudulent. In a closely-related scenario, it's possible to read an intimately autobiographical poem and not *feel confessional* at all.

Surprisingly, this holds true even in the clinical context. When I worked in psychiatric hospital units, I found clients would "share" poems that detailed all sorts of abuse or emotion they could never "tell" the group. Psychoanalytic art therapy calls this depersonalising, distancing capacity to symbol formation –

"symbol" here means *both* the use of such literary tropes as metaphor *and* the actual making of a version on paper – a "scapegoat transference". The *text* takes the blame. If challenged, the writer can say, 'It's only a poem', screw up the paper and throw it in the bin. And mental health care's no special case. Many a "public" poet has used the same line to gloss an indiscretion of the kind U.A. Fanthorpe snaps in her portrait of 'The Poet's Companion', who 'Must sustain with grace / [...] camera's curious peeping / When the Poet is reading a particularly // Randy poem about her, or (worse) about someone else'.[15] Yet this customary distancing remains curiously overlooked, not only by wives but by those readers, or critics, who like to identify poet with poem in an old-fashioned, pre-Barthesian way.[16] Confessional poets are made particularly vulnerable by this shrinkage of poetics to person. Anne Stevenson has accused Anne Sexton of writing a 'therapoetry [which] looks inward like psychoanalysis and seeks to uncover the poisonous sewers buried in the mind';[17] Sharon Olds, celebrated for repeated explorations of childhood abuses, refused until recently to acknowledge that her material might be autobiographical. This despite the substantial literature on the importance of reading poetry as artistic strategy rather than symptom: for what makes confessional verse possible is precisely the estranging effect of the poem upon its own material.

These examples of authorial detachment resonate strikingly with my experiences as a musician. Musical performance is 'impersonal' in a sense much like Eliot's:

> [...] the poet has, not a 'personality' to express, but a particular medium, which is only a medium and not a personality, in which impressions and experiences combine in peculiar and unexpected ways.[18]

However exploratory the rehearsal, in concert a fine interpretation floats free of self-consciousness. In fact, the whole effort of performance is to remove that self which might make a barrier (for example, by making mistakes or inserting mannerisms) between audience and music: while at the same time consciously continuing to make stylistic choices and follow cues. It's a bit like taking dictation, and it's no coincidence that there's an analogy with the idea some commentators have of writing poetry as a kind of translation. As Jay Parini says, '[…] poets translate from silence itself, finding a language adequate to their experience, moving yet another fragment of the unsaid into "said" territory'.[19]

Michael Donaghy was probably the best-known contemporary poet to identify this impersonal, performative character within poetry. Yesterday we caught a glimpse of silence as an anti-poem, something that threatens to overcome the text. But one way to deal with that apparent danger may be to appropriate silence as a *tabula rasa*, a stage that is *ready for* language rather than simply staging ('producing') its absence. In his essay *Wallflowers*, Donaghy evokes a kinship between poetry and dancing, which he sees as choreographing space – the dance-hall floor – rather than as individual self-expression. For Donaghy, it is the pediscript *outlining* the dance, rather than dancing *itself*, which provides a way to think about abstract form. This 'diagram', like 'the unconscious effect of form', is a kind of 'frame or scaffolding', 'really no different from the compass and map of our own expectations as readers' which falls away, in Donaghy's vision, from the actual poem: perhaps by falling away in terms of significance.[20] But if these non-subjective shapes do exist, then they must do so not only as a diagram or explanation but also *within* the dance or poem itself. The ratio that measures a piece must also be in that piece. The poem must *articulate* such forms *along with* the poet's intent. The poem is thus a form of intentional/structural *cohabitation*. We could call these forms, revealed by that impersonality which seems to underpin performance, the poem's *temporal architecture*. And these shapes made in the medium of time are a third way in which abstraction seems to occur in poetry.

Our eye-bound, screen-led culture finds it easier to conceptualise abstract form in space than time. From National Trust garden visits to Channel 4's *Grand Designs*, we've been trained in the satisfactions of visual abstraction: tall spikey plants look good behind something massy, windows affect the feel of a room, and so on. We even manage, despite the British cantankerousness around modernism, to see beauty, or at least character beyond utility, in the Sage Centre, or the view across London's Millennium Bridge to the cupcake of St Paul's. So it's both liberating and simplifying to find that we can conceptualise abstract form as existing in time *in the same way* that it exists in space. When the twentieth-century French philosopher Henri Lefebvre, attempting to reconcile 'mental' and 'real' space, claimed that: 'A spatial work (monument or architectural project) attains a complexity fundamentally different from the complexity of a text, whether prose or poetry. [...W]hat we are concerned with here is not texts but texture', he was forgetting that the poem *is not* a block of marks on a page, but an aural entity and a mental event, which is performed through time.[21] For, in calling architecture 'frozen music', Johann Wolfgang von Goethe was rearticulating an idea that already had a long history.[22] Plato, Plotinus, St Augustine and St Aquinas all suggest that the same ratios necessarily please both eye and ear.

The Renaissance architect Leon Battista Alberti said, 'I conclude that the same numbers by means of which the agreement of sounds affect our ears with delight are the very same which please our eyes and our minds.'[23] A century later, Andrea Palladio used musical ratios to give his buildings harmonious proportions. Since eighteenth-century Palladian style is named for his neo-Classicism, it's no surprise to find the golden section, apparent in so much of that architecture, underpinning harmoniousness in music as well as buildings. The golden section's proportional division is such that the ratio between the small and large quantities is the same as that between the larger quantity and the whole: approximately equal to 1.6180339887. Consecutive numbers in the Fibonacci sequence roughly mimic the golden section, becoming more accurate as the series progresses: 0, 1, 1, 2, 3, 5, 8, 13, 21, 34, 55, 89, 144, 233, 377, 610, 987, 1597 etc. Though "hidden" or encoded forms seem to be beside the point here, golden section conspiracy theories involve the usual modernist suspects: Claude Debussy, Erik Satie, Béla Bartók.[24] However, the frequency with which the 1.62 ratio recurs throughout the classical repertoire suggests that we might better understand it as so ubiquitous, so culturally powerful, that it has become significant at least for that reason, even if for no other. A recognition factor of this kind offers the listener a sensation of familiarity, something like a sense of direction or of "home".

For the classically-trained violinist, the "home" form is the sonata, which dominates Classical and Romantic repertoire.[25] Early in his or her musical formation, this structure (not itself far from the golden section in its proportions) introduces as axiomatic the principle that it is musical materials, and the relations between them, that generate music. You can't have the whole piece that will develop without the opening theme. This is that very *working itself out* through time that is such a feature of poetry's linearity, and which liberates the poem, or music, into impersonality. 'Words move, music moves, / Only in time'[26] and, given modernism's analogous sense of the text as material to be worked with, and to work itself out, it's perhaps no coincidence that, while Eliot takes on the exploded sonata form of the late Beethoven quartets, Basil Bunting's 'Sonatas', including *Briggflatts*, are based on early sonata form. Ezra Pound described *Ulysses* as a sonata, while Louis Zukofsky's *A* uses Bach and medieval song developmentally; which is sonata technique.

Of course, to point out that poetry's not independent of time is almost meaningless, since neither is anything else (except an object of metaphysical or mathematical speculation). But to suggest that it *performs* itself through time is immediately to ascribe a non-random, connective shape to that temporal movement. And without such a connection, how would each word be part of the same poem? Frozen at any single moment, a poem would be nothing more than a phoneme, lacking both form and sense. Its architectural quality is formed through time, in other words, just like music's: whether that is melody (as we observed yesterday), or a series of harmonic imperatives like Bach's (as we saw earlier). Despite the denotative functions of language, this structural relationship with time means that poetic form, like musical structure, can be built from mathematical proportions, or other *pre-semantic* forces such as escalation or closure, without posing any threat to the metrical or expressive functions of a poem – since abstraction is by definition not competing for *those* stakes. This categorical difference allows their poetic cohabitation.

The impersonal character of performance identifies and enables poetry's abstract architecture. But abstraction and impersonality overlap in another way too. Abstraction is often characterised, by both admirers and detractors, as standing at a particular distance from individual human experience. This isn't a matter of scale; or not entirely. Complaints levelled against modernist architecture, for example, often have to do with the way it fails to meet standards of lived human usefulness: le Corbusier's *Ville radieuse* generated vertical slums. Yet, though abstraction may therefore resist *individual* experience, it doesn't have to be *inhuman*. Indeed, the reverse is arguably true, as we see if we return to Michael Donaghy's vision of the performative nature of poetry. When Donaghy and others speak their poems from memory, dispensing with the scaffolding of book and lectern, they don't remove the de-personalising mask of the text, but secure it more firmly. A performer's extra-textual gestures – such as turning a page, or putting on reading glasses – stage the distance their presence creates. When this sense of an intervening reader is replaced by a poem spoken as if directly from memory, we hear only text. And it's paradoxically precisely such impersonality that enables a more human experience. The absence of the performing personality is what *makes room for* each individual audience member to make the poem their own, without being star-struck.

So human meaning and abstract form aren't inimical. Yet the exact terms of their relationship are often mysterious. For example, the sonnet's octet:sestet is both proportionate, and yet just unequal enough to cause the topple which we recognise as its turn. We might think of the form as posing – and then resolving – the problem of duality; to put it another way, of relationships. But why has the culture settled on this *precise* proportion for such semantic transformation? Why not balance a sonnet between ten lines and six, or seven and five? What makes eight:six so right? We don't kiss and make up an average of three times out of every four; nor take three-quarters as long to divorce as to marry. Pythagoreans might respond that the mathematical ratio of 8:6 is in some way *productive* of change. After all, 4:3 is the ratio of a perfect fourth in music, and Pythagoras called this pivotal interval, located between the fourth and third steps of the harmonic series, the *diatesseron*.[27] But, as we saw at the outset, that begs a further series of metaphysical, ultimately extra-textual, questions about the status of such forms in the world around us.

So the jury may be out on why *particular* formal properties structure a poem, creating what we might call its *unfrozen architecture*. But it would be hard to deny the evidence that they do co-exist with the sense we intend to make – or indeed that they can be *appropriated to* our human meaning. It's easy to trace how the sonnet turns its mass of material like a haybale, while *terza rima*'s looping, loping intellectual pace spells out the connectivity inherent in a journey. And searching out this kind of preverbal, abstract structure is arguably even more revelatory in poetry that doesn't use traditional forms, and that might otherwise be dismissed as unmusical, or not consciously organised. For example, we can see that the 'and then... and then' intrinsic to Alice Oswald's long river poems, *Dart* and *A Sleepwalk Down the Severn*, is mimetic. Deep form lets both eye and ear map the development of argument in the work of poets, like Ted Hughes, who use strophes to paragraph distinct thematic materials.[28]

In short, awareness of abstract form allows us to pitch our critical ear beyond habitual loyalties, and hear structures that underlie, and lend necessity to, the great variety of existing poetics. An awareness of deep form is of practical use in writing and redrafting, too. Every writer knows the experience of suddenly needing twice as many words to sort out a "smudge" of ambiguity. Sometimes that opens a window of breathing-space around which the earlier and later parts of the poem settle more comfortably in place; at others it distorts the whole so that we *feel* the need for remedial balancing. Making proportion conscious turns such *feelings* into serious artistic strategies. For poets do compose 'on the lips': but they also compose by ear. And the sophisticated, often preverbal, awareness this entails –

of underlying movements, of tension and release, or of making a proportionate shape in temporal space – is itself musical. Our ears are homesick for these deep-seated pleasures. They add, to mere semantic utility, something that we might call coherence, plenitude or even grace.

THIRD LECTURE

How strange the change...

> ...*but how strange the change from major to minor*
> *Every time you go away...*
> COLE PORTER, 'Every Time You Go Away'

> *Secular music has long displayed the very free use of chromaticisms similar to the modern style of writing.*
> C.H. PARRY in *Grove's Musical Dictionary*, 1879, quoted in *OED*

I'd like to start today with a quote from Robert Hughes:

> One does not read Rothko's tiers and veils of paint primarily as form: they are vehicles for colour sensation [...] almost voluptuous in their wholehearted abandonment to feeling.[1]

This great Australian art critic is too intelligent to fall for the emotional fallacy that Rothko is simply *expressing himself*. Instead, what his – we might call it a classical reading – evokes is the preverbal, sensual quality of what Hughes calls 'colour sensation', and which I'm going to call *chromaticism*.

The product of a classical discipline myself, I notice how I revert to an instinctively sensory approach when faced with art forms I know little about; relishing what Virginia Woolf calls the 'halo of the unconscious', that swirl of sensation sometimes dressed up as mysticism or the numinous. And this relish seems to me very much to the point. Chromaticism may be pre-eminently sensory but it's neither meaningless, nor meaningful in the conventional, denotative sense. Instead, today I want to argue that what it celebrates and reveals is the *experiential* nature of all the arts: the what *goes on* in viewer, listener or reader that art produces.

We've seen that music is implicated in poetry by the melodic line, as well as at the temporal level where both genres *act out* abstract form. Intuitively, though, we mean something more than either of these things when we talk about how *musical* a poem is. That 'something' has to do with *feel* – with texture. *Never mind the width, feel the quality*, as the old music-hall gag has it. So far, poetry has emerged as something that goes on – on the breath, through time – and that also goes on *in* or *to* its audience. Now I want to turn to the fuzzy surface of readerly apprehension itself, and look at how poetry speaks to it.[2]

Gwyneth Lewis's *A Hospital Odyssey* is a book-length, narrative poem, and in the following extract we pick up its characters and action in *medias res*. Maris's husband has life-threatening cancer, and in Book Two the couple encounter the New Age mood police:

> Maris rushed forward, found she was held
> by green-robed minions, 'Are you mad?
> Why are those frightening nurses veiled?
> Why shouldn't a man be furious, then sad,
> about his illness?' 'I forbid,' thundered the druid,
>
> 'negativity.' He made to plunge
> his sword into the heart. 'He must vibrate
> to higher frequencies.' Then Maris lunged
> at the doctor, scattering initiates.
> 'Kill me, then,' she screamed, 'because I hate
>
> his cancer. And you're a bunch of fakes
> and charlatans.' She overturned a tray
> of instruments. 'You're nothing like
> a real doctor. This isn't *Peace*, it's a fantasy
> of mind over matter. I want reality,
>
> not props and magic.' 'Take him away!'
> commanded the druid, then mocked, 'Go ahead!
> The evil inside you will have its day.
> Your husband, bitch, is as good as dead.'
> Maris charged at him. He fled.[3]

This is a highly disobedient cancer poem, its diction coloured by the explicit stakes – 'frightening', 'furious', 'sad', 'illness' 'evil', 'dead' – which inform not only vocabulary but the choice, not of image but of metaphorical device. The 'druid' with the 'sword' could have stepped out of the sci-fi scenario an earlier passage makes of the contemporary hospital. But for this Welsh poet he must also represent inflexible, irrational authority, first dreamt up not by a thousand hippies but by a sometimes punitively traditional national culture.[4] Yet Lewis carries off this intensity with an understated, loping metre – fundamentally iambic, its irregular numbers of feet bound together by strict *ababb* rhyme – which doesn't intrude but instead allows her story to build momentum over the long haul (at a hundred and fifty pages, the book is double the length of many poetry collections).

Another, roughly contemporary, poem that "does length" is Alice Oswald's pamphlet-length *A Sleepwalk Down the Severn*. In one palimpsest:

> all you crabs in the dark alleys of the wall
> all you mudswarms ranging up and down
> I notice you are very alert and worn out
> skulking about and grabbing what you can
>
> listen this is not the ordinary surface river
> this is not river at all this is something
> like a huge repeating mechanism
> banging and banging the jetty
>
> very hard to define, most close in kind
> to the mighty angels of purgatory
> who come solar-powered into darkness
> using no other sails than their shining wings [5]

Unbroken by the kind of conventional punctuation which, as W.S. Merwin has it, risks 'stapling' a poem to the page, this muscles onward, piling presence on presence ('crabs...wall... mudswarms'). But Oswald also renders the felt, personal movement of an individual pedestrian, through a metre whose feet vary in both number and form. Monosyllables and significant words carry the stresses: 'to the míghty ángels of púrgatory', or 'I nótice yóu are véry alért and wórn out' (listen to how that spondee 'worn out' applies its mimetic brake to the dactyl that 'very a-' leads the ear to expect). Like every concatenation of sound and sense, this fixes the lines and makes them seem unassailable; while *at the same time* expressing a to-and-fro of inflection, a kind of hesitation, that mimes the very processes of discovery and reflection the poem describes. Oswald's assonantal vocabulary, in which her *as* – 'banging and banging… angels of purgatory… solar… darkness… sails than' – push repeatedly, like the estuarial tide, against the clipped silhouettes of 'jetty… define … kind… mighty… using… their shining wings', recalls the honest-Joe diction of the later Hughes (from, for example, *River* onwards). (John Kinsella goes further, seeing assonance in itself as a *sfumato* technique which blurs and drags the sounds of the words into each other.)[6] On the other hand it's unsurprising, given that she studied in the US, to hear behind Lewis's writing the flattened, intelligent chatter of much late twentieth-century American poetry, from James Merrill to Amy Clampitt.

What most distinguishes these vertically sliced poetics, in other words, is neither function nor genre, but *texture and colour*. Several textual elements group themselves here: diction including metre, vocabulary, rhyme and its variants; register; and mood. Musicians tend to discriminate somewhat more, using the term *texture* "vertically", to refer to counterpoint and also to how much is going on within the melody, while *colour* generally indicates tonality, mood, instrumentation, key, harmony and dissonance. Form, such as fugue, does not of itself add "colour" but, despite the *qualitative* differences between them as compositional strategies, *both* instrumentation (think of, say, the exuberant efflorescence of tubular bells, triangle and brass of the 'Viennese Musical Clock' in Zoltán Kodály's *Háry János Suite*) and diatonic chromaticism – in other words, which notes are used (in, for example, Claude Debussy's piano *Préludes*) – create the *effect* which we call *colour sensation*. Chromaticism is, after all, essentially effect: the English Natural philosophers John Locke and George Berkeley had called colour a 'secondary quality' at the turn of the seventeenth and eighteenth centuries.[7]

All the same, at one moment Western music did allow itself to be guided by these sensational elements. Emerging roughly concurrently with Imagism – an era which had itself been preempted by the precocious Arthur Rimbaud's synaesthetic 'Voyelles' sonnet – Chromaticism squeezed its way out of Romanticism in the early twentieth century. By now, Late Romantics like Wagner and Mahler had stretched the old diatonic framework as far as it would go, and classical music was having to sustain such extremes of extension and ornamentation that the balance of harmonic power was changed, and with it the whole logic of musical progression. Though in fact chromaticism had been audibly pushing the boundaries of classical form since at least middle-period Brahms and the late great Beethoven quartets, in this era chromatic music was built with pitches and progressions not related through the scientific, or theoretical, cycle of fifths but appealing directly to the ear. The later French chromaticist Olivier Messiaen would sum up this radical shift when he said that, 'The classical chords have attractions and resolutions. My chords are colours. They engender intellectual colours which evolve along with them.'[8]

Synaesthetic metaphor, which gives chromaticism its name, is also at work in talk about jazz, whose "blue notes" are those tasty, disobedient sevenths, ninths and thirteenths that both expand, and seem to transgress, the harmonic series. Yet in a way such terms are meaningless. After all, every piece of music has *some* pitch colour. What chromaticism really names is the being led by feel and the senses *instead of* form and logic.[9] And in this sense – given that *all* creativity is by its nature a-systemic, the product of unpreemptable individual choice – the composition of both music and poetry is always *inherently* chromatic. Neither authorial intent nor any other factor (such as tradition or form) can overdetermine it.[10] This doesn't make chromaticism specifically *poetic*. But poetry does privilege particular non-denotative elements – sonic pleasure, aural and semantic play – incorporating them through form and rhetoric. And these elements are also present in verse at a yet more fundamental level. There's a peculiarly large margin between what a poem *says it does* – its denotative and formal content – and its total *effect*. (This roughly corresponds to, but is not, the margin between intention and accomplishment.) To an exceptional degree among literary forms, what characterises a poem *ain't what you do but the way that you do it*. Even when rhymes are part of a given form, for example, the pleasure and the point lie in how the poem produces them – what it *chooses*. The way a poem proceeds by feel rather than system is (literally) written in to the practice. I suspect that, as is so often the case, there may be a link between this profoundly *voluntary* character and (reading) *pleasure*; and I'll devote the rest of this lecture to poetry's chromatic aspects, which I see as clustered in six main areas.

The first of these is *semiotic independence*. It's fashionable to hear the play of sound, not as an unanchored quality of language itself, but as necessarily – or at least residually – denotative. It's if we can't really bear the medium's resistance to our own "desire lines", the ways we want it to be useful *to us*; or else we have a utopian vision of how transparent language should be. For Don Paterson, for example, phonemes don't just differentiate (though this is one of the functions he ascribes to consonants) but enact meanings:

> Consider, say, a mother's frustrated demand to her child, 'Put down the cup.' It's easy to separate out the four vowels | ʊ | αʊ | ɪ | ʌ | ('oo – ow – ih – uh') then imagine the first vowel pitched high to indicate urgency, the second dipping down an interval of a fifth or sixth to reinforce the impression of sane control, the third pitched identically to the first to reinforce the imperative, and the last rising another fifth – and increased in loudness – to convey the non-negotiability and frustration of the demand. The emotional sense would be clear from such a performed sequence of tones, if not the literal sense; but the consonants *pt dn th cp* alone will give us a fair stab at the semantic content, if not the tonal shape.[11]

Yet, if we listen to what happens when sound explicitly takes the stage, it's impossible to ignore the way the semiotic overpowers the semantic: in other words, the struggle they play out between them for the territory they hold in common. For example, no matter how many times I listen to a recording of Les Murray reading his 'Bats' Ultrasound', I can't catch all the words. And I don't do much better with his "bat English" on the page:

ah, eyrie-ire, aero hour, eh?
O'er our ur-area (our era aye
ere your raw row) we air our array
err, yaw, row wry – aura our orrery,
our eerie ü our ray, our arrow.

A rare ear, our aery Yahweh.[12]

But compare a passage taken pretty much as random from David Harsent, that master of internal *and internalised* rhyme and assonance:

The Duffel Bag

God's blood beads on the tarmac and something rough is boiling up
just this side of the vanishing-point, so it's probably time to get

off this stretch of blacktop and into the wayside bar, where every cup
runneth over and you breast a thickening fret

of stogie-smoke to get to the dank back room where a high stakes game
turns against you despite your trey of jacks, and soon enough

you're in way over your head with nothing and no one to blame
but the luck you've been getting since first you threw your stuff

into a duffel-bag and hooked up with the halt and lame,
with the grifters and drifters, the diehards, the masters of bluff,

the very bastards, in fact, who are lifting the last of your stash...[13]

Of course, there's an *abab* end-rhyme across these couplets. But notice, also, how 'dank back... stakes... jack', chiming within the space of just two lines, make an affect accelerator; how the knotted assonance of the last two lines quoted here mimetically cross-stitches 'diehards... bastards... // last of your stash' with 'grifters... drifters... // lifting' into a mutual inescapability; and how assonance and alliteration crowd close up and personal at 'lifting the last of your stash'. When Harsent deploys the sonic alongside the semantic, in other words, he stages a separation of language powers that's every bit as explicit as Murray's: and he does so in order to have them *reinforce* each other.

This striking, and paradoxical, reunification of elements suggests that the semiotic (the element of pure sound in language) *can* convey meanings and feelings; and that these may differ from the ones language *denotes*. (What, then, should we make of the 'Babble' computer programme, which generates "poems" by sound?) Much French psychoanalytic philosophy has gone into identifying this distinction. In her clinical practice, Julia Kristeva observed that the closer a patient gets to articulating what's really troubling them, the less fluent they become.[14] Under pressure, language stops its grammatical forward march and becomes a 'rolling English road' of repetition, hedge phrasing, stumble and malapropism. For Kristeva, this 'play', or give, in language represents an inadvertent, psychotic return to prelinguistic infancy, in which the child's babble (*lalation*) doesn't *denote* anything but *is* pure experiential play. In other words, we lapse away from signification into sound when under stress; and though this sound-play is involuntary it's not *accidental* or *insignificant*. (In fact, this applies to meaning too: it's the mechanism of parataxis, the Freudian slip.)

Kristeva's notion of the *semiotic chora*, a sensual bubble of bondedness between mother and infant in which nothing is yet divided into the conceptual entities that are building blocks of language, may be an idealised, theoretical picture. But it is *empirically* true both that children have problems learning to handle their own agency – the 'terrible twos' – and that noises like humming and bubble-blowing are non-denotative ways in which a baby occupies and pleases herself. We could imagine him or her producing a halo of sound; a kind of aural Ready-Brek, part insulation, part self-extension. And its *extra*-ness, this part left over for pleasure, the *play* in language – and other things – is what the French sexily call *jouissance*.[15] It's also what essentialist feminists like Hélène Cixous and Luce Irigaray contrast with the 'phallogocentrism' of baldly denotative language, the singular view-point of a traditionally unquestioned and unquestioning masculine authority.[16]

And here I proceed with care. Certainly, the *logos*, naming and policing the world, is foundational to the Abrahamic worldview – in Genesis 2, XIX, 'and whatsoever Adam called every living creature, that *was* the name thereof' – in which protagonists are largely male. But gender essentialism is tricky; its capacity for own goals pretty much limitless. After all, female librarians do catalogue, and male poets play with sound. On the other hand, it's also true that semiotic play *need* not indicate a psychotic return to infancy: don't we often enjoy it as a sign of high spirits, especially in children? And becoming aware of sound as a disobedient, labile, linguistic bonus – a principle of give and take, of flexibility and local il/logic within language – is clearly useful in thinking about poetry.

So there are some fruitful aspects to the idea of linguistic *jouissance*. And in fact *plenitude*, since it characterises our *experience* of sound in general, is a second manifestation of chromaticism. Sound has the generosity of an element we can't come to the end of. It's the context within which everyone with hearing lives continuously: I can always *look away now*, but I can't *listen away*. So it's not surprising that we've developed sophisticated, purely aural forms of awareness, including the ability to respond to non-verbal, intonational prompts such as the supportive or disapproving "um", or to the soothing effect of lullaby. This rich and continually-renewed aural experience may be what allows us to "get" much of what music – and poetry – does. Certainly, the ear has no trouble understanding how the alexandrine amplifies the line in Rimbaud's *Bateau ivre* like that poem's dreamt-of horizon, or how the alliterative clatter and assonantal straight-talk of a Charles Causley ballad take the reader straight back to nursery rhyme and playground din.

A related strategy is a sort of semiotic doubling that *evokes the evocative power* of these sonic cues. One famous example is the 'dreamy divagation' of Elizabeth Bishop's old couple chatting on the bus before they've seen 'The Moose':

> 'Yes...' that peculiar
> affirmative. 'Yes...'
> A sharp, indrawn breath,
> half groan, half acceptance,
> that means 'Life's like that.
> We know *it* (also death).' [17]

This passage establishes complicity with the reader by portraying both our ability to understand such cues and – as Bishop goes on to imagine 'down in the kitchen, the dog / tucked in her shawl' – their *associations* for us. We understand it by understanding how sound associations work for us. This strategy can also move beyond simple observation, deploying readerly susceptibility as a form of textual imaginative capacity: as in Billy Collins's poem 'Books', which starts with a 'library humming in the night, / a choir of authors murmuring inside their books / […] together forming a low, gigantic chord of language', and ends, 'we have to listen hard to hear the voices / of the boy and his sister receding into the woods'.[18]

As this suggests a third, and key, facet of chromaticism is *affect*: not the expression, but an acknowledgement or description, of (emotional) response; or of something that evokes such a response. (The affect, in other words, is all the reader's.) In this tricky territory, there's a fine aesthetic line between effect and manipulation. Of course, sometimes we know we're being manipulated. Leonard Cohen's cheerful cynicism, in 'Hallelujah', makes us smile in part because lyrics and setting are so 'perfectly pitched' to each other:

> I've heard there was a secret chord
> that David played, and it pleased the Lord.
> […]
> It goes like this, the fourth, the fifth
> The minor Fall, the major lift,
> The baffled king composing, hallelujah[19]

And U.A. Fanthorpe is perceptive on the true usefulness of sentimental manipulation in 'Patience Strong': 'And *See*, he said, *this is what keeps me going.*'[20] You don't need her emotional intelligence, though, to notice the tendency of a poet like Mary Oliver to tread the boundary between fine, riskily metaphysical poetry and slack-jawed homily:

> Love sorrow. She is yours now, and you must
> take care of what has been
> given.
>   ('Love Sorrow')[21]

Though Oliver can, and often does, sound more like late, great Miłosz, there's something ersatz about passages like this, which race towards a sentiment they don't seem quite patient enough to evoke by *poetic* strategies. Like *Desiderata* on a tea-towel, or Shaker style in fitted kitchens, they miss the meaning, and in so doing forfeit the thing itself.[22]

But not all deliberately conjured affect is manipulative. Poetic register is necessary – both important and intrinsic – after all. Think how each word of a late Plath poem like, say, 'Lesbos' seems to be hair-raisingly on stilts: 'Viciousness in the kitchen!' Or how his relationship to blank verse lends Sean O'Brien's work a level-pegging, historically-grounded, authority: so it never sounds like special pleading, whether for communities saddled with Thatcher's post-industrial legacy or – in elegies such as those for Barry MacSweeney, or Thom Gunn – individual emotion. If it contributes to register, vocabulary also colours in other, more obvious, ways: through ingenious, metaphorical usage or the frisson of the unusual, particularly loan-words and dialect. 'The Obligatory Dialect Poem' in Toby Martinez de las Rivas's pamphlet (*Faber New Poets 2*) is fair play on, for example, John Glenday's *Grain*, Robin Robertson's *The Wrecking Light*, Don Paterson's *Rain* and Fiona Benson's *Faber New Poets 1*.

Often, what complicates affect isn't so much the way it's used or mis-used as its reception. What we might call the Emotional School of Reader Response holds that whatever a poem says expresses what its author's feeling. Leaving aside the paucity of this picture of both literary craft and language, it's a strangely innocent position to adopt. Have these readers never found themselves telling a lie? But non-poets do tend in general to read register in literal ways: to *believe* it, as it were. Plath's verse is the exemplar: trailing its notorious comet's tail of reception, by psychoanalytic critics like Susan Kavaler-Adler as well as literary critics who should know better, as symptomology rather than conscious poetics. I suspect this is because register is entry level: it's *where the reader comes in*, in every sense. A unifying poetic trope, it tends to be present (at least in germ) from the first line, while other "colour sensations" – intensification, abstraction, musical clustering, even emotional message – may appear and disappear in the course of a poem. But it's also entry-level in the sense of being easily apparent: one of those primitive cues our brains respond to, as if *before* conscious thought.

If affect can seem to orchestrate the whole body of a poem, it does at least work with the grain of that whole, following the poem's trajectory. But chromaticism can also operate, fourthly, in a palimpsest, as a burst of "vertical" experience. In music, instrumentation can create an inflection that's both aural and symbolic – we feel *and* understand it – by means of what I'll call *iconic chromaticism*. For example, the flute J.S. Bach used in setting the *'Crucifixus est'* of his *B Minor Mass* would have been made of bone, serving as a *memento mori* with which to "play dead". The purely mimetic tolling tubular bells of Hector Berlioz's 'March to the Scaffold' are upstaged by four brass bands in his *Grand Messe des Morts*: since brass instruments represent both martial music and the last trump.[23] Within each tradition, poetic form offers similar symbolic opportunities: a sonnet always refers to love, even if to the potential loss of all that one loves (John Donne's 'Death be not Proud'); or else it uses that affective freight to add weight to a poem about, for example, place (William Wordsworth's 'On Westminster Bridge') or politics (Percy Bysshe Shelley's 'England in 1819'). These *iconic* functions of form are additional to their intrinsic *technical* properties. They function, like an iconostasis, to *display the direction of the gaze* rather than perform the functions of that towards which it's directed. In other words, just as the iconostasis represents what it conceals, iconic form stands in for what we don't directly *hear*.

Musical key can also be used iconically: as when the names of notes spell out a message. The collaborative *FAE Sonata* for violin and piano, by Brahms, Schumann and Albert Dietrich, is built on the mnemonic for their Romantic motto, *Frei aber einsam* (*Free but alone*). J.S. Bach used B A C H (H is B♭ in North European notation) in his late, unfinished *The Art of Fugue*, and this progression has since been used, as a homage, by composers as disparate as Schumann, Liszt, Rimsky-Korsakov, Webern and Arvo Pärt. Operating only within the music's *scoring*, and not its sound – since even if you have perfect pitch and can recognise the F, for example, you're simply *identifying* the customary name for a sound, not *hearing that name itself* – *this* kind of iconicity finds its best analogy in concrete poetry. The line-breaks of George Herbert's 'Easter Wings' are both displayed *and* enacted – rhyme making their "flight" of rise and fall, as well as the shape of their fanned wings, audible:

>   Lord, Who createdst man in wealth and store,
>   Though foolishly he lost the same,
>   Decaying more and more,
>   Till he became
>   Most poore:
>   With Thee
>   O let me rise,
>   As larks, harmoniously,
>   And sing this day Thy victories:
>   Then shall the fall further the flight in me.[24]

Yet the "sonnets" of performance poet Patience Agbabi's 'Problem Pages', fourteen-line blocks of justified text, are a form that exists purely in print.[25]

Perhaps this simply highlights something paradoxical in the nature of scoring itself. Though we might think of it as a musical or textual "service stairs", the score is often how we first approach a work. Between the seventeenth and nineteenth centuries, musical scores moved from recording information about how to perform a piece – the figured bass – to a transcription of how it should sound in performance.[26] Poetry's analogous journey can be seen as leading from orality to non-lineated Classical and Anglo-Saxon inscriptions in abbreviated (or even runic) script, and on to fully-laid-out print – and today's preoccupation with forms of reproduction, both digital and live, which dispense with written text altogether. These changes not only echo the shift from specialist expertise to the point where general literacy means everyone can read – and is therefore the *defining* audience for – a poem. They also change what a poem *is* in an important way. When the poem on the page scores the whole sound of a poem, *the way it goes*, there's no longer any space in which the poem exists *as distinct from* how it sounds. And this overlap, or tension, between *score and performance* houses the semiotic "rub" (fetishised in music by the use of "authentic instruments"). The non-identity of these modes of presentation of the very same poetic material necessarily leaves a kind of give, or doubling, at the heart of its identity. This surplus – which is *how the poem sounds* – is *activated* every time it's performed: whether that's in a public reading or as someone reads a page to themselves.

But it poses puzzles too. Is the musical *ur-text* the autograph manuscript, that object sunk in eighteenth-century paperiness, fragile and sometimes almost illegible: or the "definitive" performance by a Solti or a Karajan? When, for example in a seminar, someone else reads a poet's signature poem but fails to insert his or her characteristic inflections, is that automatically their failure, a failure of the poet's scoring – or no failure at all? And how does this differ from the way that a company of actors "score" a text, working out the timings – the rhythm – of a performance entailed by the text but not determined by it?

It seems that poetry is *inherently public*. Just as singing is willy-nilly out loud, so a composed poem, in "coming out" as a *language act* rather than remaining in thought, is inherently communicative. It posits someone beyond the author. In David Harsent's 'The Duffel Bag', we saw assonance and internal rhyme form a cat's cradle of congruence, which not only contains and guides the reader (or audience) but produces the *sound of integration*. Harsent himself has made the point that such integration *is established through, and establishes*, readerly complicity. In the example he gives, when rhyme prompts us to complete the famous couplet in Shelley's 'The Mask of Anarchy', we also complete – that is, at some level assent to – the poem's *sentiment* that 'I met Murder on the way – / He had a mask like Castlereagh.'[27]

Sixthly, then, as it builds on pleasure or expectation, *even by disrupting them*, chromaticism establishes complicity with the reader. And this private, experiential and *direct* relationship between those as it were consenting adults, the poem and the reader, offers a radical alternative to the fashionably reductive reading by topic which much contemporary British literature teaching – and more unforgivably reviewing – brings to poetry. Increasingly, readers, audiences and student learn that the poem is a sort of spreadsheet of ideas (and, just possibly, strategies).

But this is like preferring the programme note to the music, the bullet-point manifesto to a great orator's rhetoric: if we really believe the "explanation" is (more than) equal to the poem, we clearly don't need the stuff itself at all. Poetry's chromaticism works against the grain of this encroaching disarmament to remind us how *only the poem itself* does *being* the poem. It draws the reader's experience into the very texture of the poem itself.

As I write this, on an InterCity Express racing through snowy Austria, my gaze is repeatedly drawn to the woman opposite. With her deeply wrinkled pensioner's face, miniskirt and thigh boots, she's certainly eccentric. She holds the headphones of an old-fashioned Walkman against her ears, hands to the sides of her head as if to squeeze even closer to an experience that leaks out, anyway, in the high notes of an opera. It must be very loud. Her eyes are closed; her (ecstatic) expression is shockingly private. Who's to say why she's moved – or why by Verdi? The point is that she must listen to the thing itself – the moving soundscape that takes her with it as it happens – in order to *be* so moved. She recreates each aria as it's recreated in her: a boundaryless to-and-fro between her pleasure and the pleasurability of the music. And *this*, it seems to me, is what "goes on" at the fuzzy border of experience between self and other which is reading a poem: a deeper and perhaps older complicity than simple understanding. I suspect it's what we mean – or what we long for – when we say that poetry is *musical*.

Coda

These lectures have looked at three areas of analogy between poetry and music, and at what those analogies might suggest about, and for, poetry. My hope is that they function as thought experiments that *allow for the possibility* of unfamiliar, even unorthodox, ideas about poetics. After all (as every totalitarian knows), once ideas have been thought they tend to hang about, getting mixed up in all kinds of practice. And an underdetermined, vibrant, poetic diversity is surely our best hope of avoiding the law of diminishing returns that governs its alternative.

We've seen music imply the possibility of readdressing three aspects of poetry. Melodiousness suggests that – as in song – the spoken phrase, articulated by breath, may be rhythmically and semantically formative. The role of abstract form in poetry – formal relationships such as proportion, constructed within time just as geometrical form is constructed within space – might turn out be more fundamental, to both the individual poem and the work of poetry as a whole, even than aspects of what we normally think of as poetic form: or might be enunciated through those aspects. And "musicality" also seems to name the pleasure principle, the experience of affect or of sensory enjoyment, that characterises our relationship to a poem.

All three of these approaches make some reference to performativity. The poem they arrive at is public and shared. It belongs to the concrete world in which we are ourselves embodied. Like us, it is performed, or performs itself, through time.

But these approaches have also suggested a somewhat lateral take on poetics. Among other things, they've implied that formal metre might not be the only choice of *musical* diction; that formal relationship might be revealed in the length, or stress-distribution, of juxtaposed phrases; that structure might be built by uniting or resolving several aspects of a topic at a proportionate point, by extended metaphor, or with palimpsest material used to rhythmic effect (this rather Mahlerian technique hasn't been much seen since in Anglophone verse since David Jones and Basil Bunting); and that poems might be coloured as much by suggestion, resonance, sound-play and ornamentation as by their argument or import.

All these *mights* hardly seem prescriptive enough for a poetics. And my ambition isn't to propose one, but simply to try to clear out a few conceptual corridors and back stairs, down which poetry might move more freely for both readers and writers, true to what Hélène Cixous calls a 'strategy of velocity'.[1] I started this project by quoting Pierre Boulez's warning to self as he embarked on an exploration of Western musical fundamentals in *On Music Today*. I'll take the risk of ending with the quotation he offers, a few pages later, from Baudelaire:

> I pity the poets who are guided only by instinct; I believe them to be incomplete. [...] Somewhere in every poet there must be a critic.[2]

NOTES

PRELUDE

1. Pierre Boulez, *Boulez on Music Today*, trs. Susan Bradshaw and Richard Rodney Bennett (London: Faber & Faber, 1975), p. 11.
2. Paul de Man, *Resistance to Theory* (Minneapolis: University of Minnesota Press, 1986).
3. Frank Kermode, *Forms of Attention* (Chicago: University of Chicago Press, 1985); Donald Revell, *The Art of Attention: A Poet's Eye-view* (Minneapolis: Graywolf Press, 2007).
4. Percy Bysshe Shelley, *A Defence of Poetry*, ll. 311-20, in *Percy Bysshe Shelley: Selected Poetry and Prose*, ed. Alasdair D.F. Macrae (London: Routledge, 1991), p. 212.

FIRST LECTURE
Point Counterpoint

1. Paul Klee, tr. Paul Findlay, in *Art in Theory 1900-1990*, eds. Charles Harrison and Paul Wood (Oxford: Basil Blackwell, 1992), p. 344.
2. Its earliest example is from the late C16th. *Oxford English Dictionary* (Oxford: OUP, 1971), Vol L, p. 527.
3. These lectures deal primarily with examples from Western classical music and literary verse not because I imagine they're the best or only traditions, but because they're the ones I know about and can think from. Besides, they are culturally analogous.
4. Indeed, Stravinsky notates this group-etto, each time it occurs, as part ornament (grace notes) as well as part metrical scoring – though *rubato*, which gives the performer temporal flexibility.
5. This definition, which Derrida gave in 1970, is from *The Languages of Criticism and The Sciences of Man: The Structuralist Controversy*, eds. Richard Macksey and Eugenio Donato (Baltimore: Johns Hopkins University Press, 1972), p. 254. In early work, in particular *Of Grammatology* tr. Gayatri Chakravorty Spivak, who first brought the term into English. Later roughly analogous terms with which Derrida deconstructs the metaphysics of presence include '*arché-writing*', '*pharmakos/pharmakon*', '*specter*' and, perhaps most famously, '*difference*'. (Baltimore & London: Johns Hopkins University Press, 1976).
6. Tim Ingold, *Lines: a Brief History* (London: Routledge, 2007). Establishing a typology of lines of practice, his Chapters 1 and 5 identify speech, song and music as related practices, made material by analogous forms of notation.

7. Boulez 1975, p. 20.

8. In 1999, Richard Taruskin caused a storm by claiming to have identified specific ethnographic sources for the "folksong" material in the *Rite*, something which Stravinsky had resisted. Richard Taruskin, *Stravinsky and the Russian Traditions* (Berkeley: University of California Press, 1996). Eric Walter White describes this melody as 'borrowed from a collection of Lithuanian folk music': *Eric Walter White, Stravinsky: The Composer and his works* (Berkeley & Los Angeles: University of California Press, 1966).

9. Martin Heidegger, 'The Thinker as Poet' in *Poetry, Language, Thought*, tr. Albert Hofstadter (San Francisco: Harper, 1975), p. 13.

10. *The Oxford Companion to Music* calls 'Song' 'an instinctive activity of the human species, a natural means of self-expression common to all races. Its origins can be traced back into prehistory, most obviously to the human fascination with rhythm and the inflections of speech.' *The Oxford Companion to Music*, ed. Alison Latham (Oxford: OUP, 2002), p. 1183. Singing feels voluntary and unmediated, although the fact that it repeats a practice that has accompanied human existence since early times establishes a particular complicity between its occasions.

11. I'm grateful to John Kinsella for reminding me that tradition simply encodes the way in which we have necessary a priori knowledge of whatever forms we humans devise: since as Kant point out they must fit with our capacities.

12. Juxtaposed in Dennis O'Driscoll's highly browsable *The Bloodaxe Book of Poetry Quotations* (Tarset: Bloodaxe Books, 2006), pp. 28-29.

13. Something I tried to explore in 'Long Sight and Reading Glasses', *Poetry CXCV*, 5, February 2010, pp. 402-10.

14. Joseph Brodsky, *Collected Poems in English* (Manchester: Carcanet, 2001), pp. 163-208 and 215-225 respectively. 'Lithuanian Nocturne' starts with a sea-scene and only turns back to greet its dedicatee, the Lithuanian poet Tomas Venclova, in the second section.

15. Jacob Polley, *The Brink* (London: Picador, 2003), p. 41.

16. Jamie McKendrick, *Ink Stone* (London: Faber & Faber, 2003), p. 25.

17. Eavan Boland, *Object Lessons* (Manchester: Carcanet, 1990), p. 11.

18. In E.M. Forster, *Aspects of the Novel* (London: Penguin Classics, 2000).

19. That the work is a form unfolded through time is broadly the subject of my second lecture.

20. St Cross House Day Centre, Newport, Isle of Wight, IOWDHA, 1993.

21. I return to this in the third lecture.

22. These verses are slightly varied in the seventeenth century by the King James Bible:

> 1 The LORD is my light and my salvation; whom shall I fear? the LORD is the strength of my life; of whom shall I be afraid? [...]

4 One thing have I desired of the LORD, that will I seek after; that I may dwell in the house of the LORD all the days of my life, to behold the beauty of the LORD, and to enquire in his temple.

5 For in the time of trouble he shall hide me in his pavilion: in the secret of his tabernacle shall he hide me; he shall set me up upon a rock.

23. Olivier Messiaen in conversation with Claude Samuel, *Music and Colour*, tr. E. Thomas Glasow (Portland, OR: Amadeus Press, 1994), p. 69.

24. Douglas Dunn, *Terry Street* (London: Faber & Faber, 1969), p.20; *The Donkey's Ears* (London: Faber & Faber, 2000).

25. Philip Larkin, 'The Trees', 'The Whitsun Weddings', 'Wild Oats' in *Collected Poems*, ed. Anthony Thwaite (London: Faber & Faber and the Marvell Press, 1988), pp. 166, 114-16, 143.

26. Philip Larkin, *The Whitsun Weddings* (London: Faber & Faber, 1964), pp. 45-46.

27. In a letter to the author, 4 May 2010. I'm grateful to Anne Stevenson for her responses to this lecture.

28. Like any well brought-up feminist I, too, am uncomfortable with the somewhat essentialist terms of this passage. Better, perhaps, to think of poetry as a social behaviour, arising from normative givens.

29. John Burnside, *Waking Up in Toytown* (London: Jonathan Cape, 2010), p. 147.

30. Jorie Graham, *Overlord* (Manchester: Carcanet, 2005), p. 86.

31. Peter Kivy, *Osmin's Rage: Philosophical Reflections on Opera, Drama and Text* (Princeton, NJ: Princeton University Press, 1988).

32. As we'll see in the third lecture, this is something music routinely does through key, or chromaticism.

33. Though it was first written as an imperial anthem, '*Gott erhalte Franz den Kaiser*'.

34. Charles Olson, *Collected Prose*, eds. Donald Hall & Benjamin Friedlander (Berkeley & Los Angeles: University of California Press, 1997).

35. Hugo Ball, *Dada Manifesto*. Read at the first public Dada soirée, Zurich, 14 July 1916.

36. Lewis Carroll, *Alice's Adventures in Wonderland and Through the Looking Glass* (Harmondsworth: Puffin, 1962).

SECOND LECTURE
Here is my space

1. Tomas Tranströmer, trans. Robin Fulton, 'Romanesque Arches' in *New Collected Poems* (Tarset: Bloodaxe Books, 1997/2011), p. 158.

2. The interval between a pair of notes whose frequency ratio is 1:2

(e.g. 440 and 880 Hertz) is an octave (in this case octave As). The interval between two notes whose frequency ratio is 2:3 is a perfect fifth (for example, 440 and 660 Hz: A and the E above it); while the 3:4 ratio produces a perfect fourth (as from E upward to the next A).

3. The present, Marcatorian or Holderian, comma was first calculated by the Chinese mathematician Ching Fang in the first century BCE. In the seventeenth century, Nicholas Mercator calculated the variation between these circles of perfect fifths and perfect octaves more accurately, and William Holder pointed out that the perfect major third is also very close to being present in equal temperament. In order to enable the key relationships within an octave to ring true, these mathematicians have divided the octave into fifty-three intervals, or "commas", rather than the twelve semitones, because fifty-three consecutive perfect fifths (3/2ths to the power of 53) very nearly equals thirty-one perfect octaves (2/1ths to the power of 53). These physical facts are genuinely, if imperfectly, universal: something that seems *prima facie* difficult for poetry, with its multiplicity of local languages, to match.

4. Les Murray, *Selected Poems* (Manchester: Carcanet, 1986), pp. 51-2.

5. Although a less welcome consequence of this is arguably a dulled pitch palate. Twentieth-century composers, from Berg to Stockhausen, made a compensatory exploration not of the *expressive* qualities of discord but of how its systematic use might shift the whole project of contemporary music.

6. The relationship between the tonic and the fifth step in each musical scale – the first interval, after the octave, in the harmonic series – is that between the "home" key and its neighbour in the step-wise acquisition of key-signature sharps, then (through enharmomic modulation) shedding of flats, of key cousinship. The "cycle" includes and relates all keys and returns to its starting point.

7. John Newlands, 'On Relations Among the Equivalents', *Chemical News*, 10: 94–95, 20 August 1864.

8. In a recent BBC Radio 4 interview.

9. Gerard Manley Hopkins, *Poems and Prose*, selected and edited by W.H. Gardner (Harmondsworth: Penguin, 1979), p. 60.

10. Robin Robertson, 'Wonderland' in *The Wrecking Light* (London: Picador, 2010), p. 13.

11. William Shakespeare, 'Sonnet 18' in *The Complete Works*, ed. Peter Alexander (London & Glasgow: Collins, 1971), p. 1311.

12. 'opon': *sic, The Poems of Emily Dickinson*, ed. R.W. Franklin (Cambridge, MA: Belknap, 2005), #381, p. 175.

13. R.S. Thomas, *No Truce with the Furies* (Newcastle upon Tyne: Bloodaxe Books, 1995), p.74.

14. Pauline Stainer, *Crossing the Snowline* (Tarset: Bloodaxe Books, 2008), p. 40.

15. U.A.Fanthorpe, *Neck Verse* (Calstock: Peterloo, 1992).

16. In 'The Death of the Author' (1968), Roland Barthes pointed out that authors were no longer seen as people who had made a textual object, but as 'brands' of those 'texts'. *Image-Music-Text*, tr. Stephen Heath (New York: Hill and Wang, 1977), pp. 142-48.

17. Anne Stevenson interviewed by Charlotte Austin, 'Anne Sexton Forty Years On' in *Poetry Review*, 99:4 (December 2009), p. 59.

18. T.S. Eliot, 'Tradition and the Individual Talent' in *Selected Essays* (London: Faber & Faber, 1999), pp. 13-22.

19. Jay Parini, 'Hard, Beautiful Truths' in *Poetry Review*, 96:4 (December 2006), pp. 82-85.

20. In the example Donaghy uses, James Merrill's couplets are so internalised that Ephraim, Merrill's Ouija board "author", adopts them for his dictation in *The Changing Light at Sandover*. Michael Donaghy, *Wallflowers* (London: Poetry Society, 1999), pp. 17-20.

21. Henri Lefebvre, *The Production of Space*, tr. Donald Nicholson-Smith (Oxford: Blackwell, 1991), p. 222.

22. '*Baukunst eine erstarrte Musik nenne*', the phrase used by Goethe in *Conversations with Eckerman* (1836), appears earlier in Friedrich Wilhelm Joseph Schelling's *Philosophie der Kunst* (1802-3).

23. Leon Alberti, *On the Art of Building in Ten Books*, tr. Joseph Rykwert, Neil Leach, Robert Tavernor (Cambridge MA: MIT Press, 1999), Bk. IV, ch. 5, p. 305.

24. See for example: Erno Lendvai, *Béla Bartók: an analysis of his music* (London: Kahn & Averill, 1971), Roy Howat, *Debussy in Proportion: a musical analysis* (Cambridge: Cambridge University Press, 1983), Courtney S. Adams, 'Erik Satie and Golden Section Analysis' in *Music and Letters*, 77:2 (Oxford: Oxford University Press, 1996), pp. 242-52.

25. In sonata form, two pieces of thematic material, or subjects, are first given in distinct but related keys, then worked over, leading eventually to a restatement in which both are now in the same key, that of the first subject. Since perfect pitch suggests there is no such thing as real transposition, this means that the second subject has undergone a transformation of *character* as well as pitch.

26. T.S. Eliot, 'Burnt Norton V' in *Collected Poems 1909-1962* (London: Faber & Faber, 1985), p.194.

27. There's a qualitative difference between noticing that a particular proportion is naturally occurring, and believing that this natural occurrence confers particular metaphysical or semantic status. Arguably all we can do is resort to the old existentialist trick of being clear about the forms that are available to work with.

28. I'm grateful to John Kinsella for his discussion of Galway Kinnell's 'sense of music in the depth and reverberation of the image' in an email to me, 29 April 2010.

THIRD LECTURE
How strange the change

1. Robert Hughes, 'Mark Rothko in Babylon', *Nothing if not Critical: Selected Essays on Art and Artists* (London: Collins Harvill, 1990), p. 242.

2. There are analogies, of course, with the actions of fuzzy logic.

3. Gwyneth Lewis, *A Hospital Odyssey*, Book 2 (Tarset: Bloodaxe Books, 2010), pp. 29-30.

4. One which has often been inhospitable to this younger *woman* poet who brought "foreign" (English) forms into the language.

5. Alice Oswald, 'In a Tidal Valley' in *A Century of Poetry Review*, ed. Fiona Sampson (Manchester: Carcanet, 2009), p. 348.

6. In an email to me, 5 May 2010.

7. John Locke, *An Essay Concerning Human Understanding* (1689) and George Berkeley, *Principles of Human Knowledge* (1710). Locke, *An Essay Concerning Human Understanding*, ed. Peter H. Nidditch (Oxford: Oxford University Press, 1990). Berkeley, *Principles of Human Knowledge and Three Dialogues*, ed. Roger Woolhouse (Harmondsworth: Penguin, 1988).

8. Olivier Messiaen, *Music and Colour: Conversations with Claude Samuel*, tr. E. Thomas Glasow (Portland, OR: Amadeus Press, 1994), p. 62.

9. S.T. Coleridge used the term *synaethesia* for literary tropes that 'unite unlike things'. This is intuitively different from the way I'm using the term here.

10. We could think of the (literally) *idiom*-atic aspect of the poem as its "parapsychology", or unconscious: that is, the whole field of effect and affect that the poem brings with it by virtue of being language rather than, say, an abacus or binary code.

11. Don Paterson, 'from The Lyric Principle Part 2: The Sound of Sense' in *Century of Poetry Review*, ed. Fiona Sampson (Manchester: Carcanet, 2009), p. 337.

12. Les Murray, 'Bats' Ultrasound' in *Collected Poems* (Manchester: Carcanet, 1998), p. 368.

13. David Harsent, 'The Duffel Bag' in *Night* (London: Faber & Faber, 2011) p. 24.

14. Julia Kristeva interviewed by Sue Sellers, 'A Question of Subjectivity' in *Women's Review*, 12 (1982), pp. 19-21; Julia Kristeva, *Pouvoirs de l'horreur* (Paris: Éditions du Seuil, 1980).

15. 'At the simplest level of meaning – metaphorical – woman's capacity for multiple orgasm indicates that she has the potential to attain something more than Total, something extra – abundance and waste (a cultural throwaway), Real and unrepresentable.' Betsy Wing, definition of *jouissance* in 'Glossary' to Hélène Cixous and Catherine Clément, *The Newly-Born Woman* (Minnesota & Manchester: University of Minnesota Press and Manchester University Press, 1987), p.165.

For Luce Irigaray, it's not multiple orgasm but genital plurality that makes woman *Ce sexe qui n'en est pas un* (Paris: Minuit, 1977) and entails the semiotic element she believes women's writing is authentic to.

16. Phallus + logos + centre.

17. Elizabeth Bishop, 'The Moose' in *Complete Poems* (London: Chatto & Windus, 1991), pp. 169-173.

18. Billy Collins, 'Books' in *Taking off Emily Dickinson's Clothes* (London: Picador, 2000), pp. 11-12.

19. Leonard Cohen, 'Hallelujah' on *Various Positions* (Columbia, 1984, prod. John Lissauer).

20. U.A. Fanthorpe, 'Patience Strong' in *Selected Poems* (Harmondsworth: Penguin, 1986), p. 16.

21. Mary Oliver, *Red Bird* (Tarset: Bloodaxe Books, 2008), p. 64.

> They stay in my mind, these beautiful people
> or anyway people beautiful to me, of which
> there are so many. You, and you, and you,
> whom I had the fortune to meet, or maybe
> missed.
>
> ('In the Evening, In the Pinewoods', p. 63)

23. From *Symphonie Fantastique*, Op. 14.

24. George Herbert, 'Easter-wings' in *George Herbert*, ed. Jo Shapcott (London: Faber & Faber, 2006), p. 7.

25. Patience Agbabi, *Bloodshot Monochrome* (Edinburgh: Canongate, 2008).

26. If we think about poetry as song, we might assume that what we hear are the notes of vowels; the swell or breath of a note. Not only may vowels sound *pitched* – Gerard Manley Hopkins's vowelling-on and vowelling-off – but they seem to be the space through which a note sounds. Like the 'o' blooming and ballooning in its monosyllable, the word 'note' itself makes us think of the O written on the musical stave; of a circle to be filled with colour and timbre. Yet music is in fact notated by the *start* of each note – the strike, or puff – though this notation *includes* other information, such as pitch and duration. It's as if Western musical notation is, like the Hebrew alphabet, all consonants. For example, in Baroque-style string playing it's up to the string itself to keep the note vibrating after it's been sounded, to a much greater extent than in later schools of playing. Founded on the ability of modern instruments (differently strung, and with heavier bows) and techniques (*legato* bowing, *vibrato*) to sustain a sound, these "play through the note" to such an extent that the nineteenth century had to re-introduce the percussive element with new bowing techniques: *fouetté, staccato, spiccato, flying spiccato*.

This suggests the possibility of a consonantal poetics. After all, speech is percussion – of tongue, lips and palate – as well as breath. The clatter of alliteration, so eagerly shed by poets the moment they leave the classroom, should at least alert us to the *audibility* of consonants. And in assonantal forms like Welsh *cynghanedd*, it's the consonants which draw the veil through which the vowels work: concealment once again also acting as a projective screen. Alliteration was part of the patterning of the Finnish traditional material which became the *Kalevala*, as indeed of the Estonian *Kaevipoeg*, Old Norse, Anglo-Saxon verse including *Beowulf* and even the Middle English prosody of *Pearl* and *Piers Plowman*. Indeed, to compare the burr of assonantal poetry with the click and chime of something led by the consonants, is to be aware of how deeply integrated consonantal alertness already is – as to the difference between those two articles, 'the' and 'a'. The former is thickened, softened and anonymised by that almost-pluralising *th*, while the latter arguably sounds baldly isolate.

27. In conversation. *Percy Bysshe Shelley*, ed. Fiona Sampson (London: Faber & Faber, 2011), p. 23.

CODA

1. Hélène Cixous, *So Close*, tr. Peggy Kamuf (Cambridge: Polity, 2009), p. 21.

2. Pierre Boulez, *Boulez on Music Today*, tr. Susan Bradshaw & Richard Rodney Bennett (London: Faber & Faber, 1975), pp. 11-12.

Fiona Sampson left school at sixteen to work and study as a concert violinist. After attending the Salzburg Mozarteum and Paris Conservatoire, she was a Foundation Scholar at the Royal Academy of Music, where she won John Waterhouse Year Prize. She later studied at the Universities of Oxford, where she won the Newdigate Prize, and Nijmegen, where she received a PhD in the philosophy of language.

Her eighteen books include *Rough Music* (Carcanet, 2010), shortlisted for the 2010 Forward and T.S. Eliot Prizes. She has also been shortlisted for the Forward single poem prize, and has received Writer's Awards from the Arts Councils of England and of Wales and the Society of Authors, as well as the US *Literary Review*'s Charles Angoff Award and a Hawthornden Fellowship.

As well as collections of poetry, her books include a self-help guide, *Poetry Writing* (Robert Hale, 2009); an academic study, *Writing: Self and Reflexivity* (Palgrave, 2006) with Celia Hunt, relating critical theories to the writing process; a collection of essays, *On Listening* (Salt, 2007); and several theoretical and practical studies of writing in health care, a field she helped develop for over a decade.

Published in more than thirty languages, she has eleven books in translation including *Patuvachki Dnevnik*, awarded the Zlaten Prsten (Macedonia, 2004). From 2002 to 2005 she edited *Orient Express*, a twice-yearly volume of contemporary writing from post-communist Europe, which she founded. She has been editor of *Poetry Review* since 2005, only the second woman editor (after Muriel Spark in 1947-49) in its history. In 2009, she received a Cholmondeley Award and was elected a Fellow of the Royal Society for Literature, and will shortly serve on its Council.

She gave the Newcastle/Bloodaxe Poetry Lectures at Newcastle University in 2010, published in 2011 as *Music Lessons*. In 2011 her edition of *Percy Bysshe Shelley* (Faber) was the July Choice for the PBS Online Reading Group.

Beyond the Lyric (2012), her critical survey of contemporary British poetry, and a new collection, *Coleshill* (2013), are both forthcoming from Chatto.